Night Visit from the Grave . . .

New Orleans cab drivers avoid that city's St. Louis Cemetery #1 whenever possible. For there ... prowls a woman in white. A cabbie was hailed by her one night. He stopped for her and took her to the address that she gave him.

When they got there, she asked him to go to the door and inquire for a man who lived there. The man himself came to the door, and the driver told him of the passenger waiting within. When the man was told what she looked like, he exclaimed,

"That's my wife—she's been dead for years!"

Bantam Books by Richard Winer

THE DEVIL'S TRIANGLE
HAUNTED HOUSES (with Nancy Osborn)

HAUNTED HOUSES

BY RICHARD WINER
AND NANCY OSBORN

HAUNTED HOUSES
A Bantam Book / July 1979

2nd printing
3rd printing
4th printing

*Bantam Books are published by Bantam Books, Inc. Its trade-
mark, consisting of the words "Bantam Books" and the por-
trayal of a bantam, is Registered in U.S. Patent and Trademark
Office and in other countries. Marca Registrada. Bantam
Books, Inc., 666 Fifth Avenue, New York, New York 10019.*

PRINTED IN THE UNITED STATES OF AMERICA

Acknowledgments

There are many persons who helped with the creation of this book. Without their able assistance *Haunted Houses* would have been just another book about ghosts. They are: R. Chris Ralla, Terry Boyce and Tim Howley from the staff of *Old Cars Magazine* who got us going on the James Dean curse; Dr. Dei Wilkerson of Honolulu who put us on to the Hawaiian ghosts; Jack Burdett, West Virginia historian and authority on the Chief Cornstalk Curse; Jerry Strobel of Opry Land U.S.A.; David Paine and Terry Biega of Nashville's Metropolitan Historic Commission; Queen Dickens of the Pompano Beach, Florida Library; Clem Vitek, head librarian of the *Baltimore Sun;* Corinne Drennan and Diane Johnson of the Country Music Hall of Fame; Susie W. Hallberg at the Fredericksburg, Virginia Visitor Center; Duncan Mackenzie, columnist and historian; Marshall Wiley Hawks, curator of the Frigate *Constellation;* dozens of employees of the National Park Service; Nancy Taylor; Debbie Herrick; Randy Porter; Marge Serkin; Rose Baco; Barbara Perry; Juanita Shultz; J. Hollifield; and an anonymous (by his own choice), Coral Gables city official who arranged for us to hold a seance in the world's largest haunted house; and those many, many others whose names, but not their help, are forgotten.

Contents

Introduction

Nearly every community in the United States can claim at least one haunted house. Some have more than one. There is the small town of Casadega in central Florida with a permanent population of fewer than two hundred people which has no less than six haunted houses.

In most places the citizenry, except for a few knowledgeable individuals, is totally unaware of the fact that macabre dwellings are standing in their midst. For example, how many people in Morristown, New Jersey, are aware that one of that city's better restaurants, The Wedgewood Inn, has been haunted since early in the last century, and apparitions have been seen in the dining establishment as late as 1978 by diners and employees alike.

Most spirits or entities prefer to remain undiscovered and can be contacted by only the most talented mediums. However, many ghostly inhabitants can make living persons feel their presence. Some spirits can become visible as apparitions. Others are only heard. Many remain invisible, although their actions can be seen. Members of this group are usually referred to as poltergeists. There are incidents where entities can be felt by spiritual energies such as hot spots or cold areas. But in whatever form they take, most ghosts are harmless to the living. Some ghosts even have a sex drive and make erotic overtures to the living.

There are exceptions, however. Incidents of ghosts harming the living are rare, but they do occur. Happenings of horror, destruction and even death have been documented. These abominations have occurred in old English manor houses and castles on the Rhine as well as right here in the United States. Some of these eerie hauntings are the result of maledictions or curses when a spirit lingers to watch his blasphemous wish of evil take place.

Many readers will scoff at the existence of ghosts. However, many great people such as Abraham Lincoln, Franklin Roosevelt and Harry Truman were convinced that ghostly entities are real. In fact, at the time of his death, Thomas Edison was working on a machine with which to communicate with the dead.

Pocahontas' body, lovely as a poplar,
Sweet as a red haw in November
Or a paw paw in May,
Did she wonder? Does she remember? . . .
In the dust, in the cool tombs?

Carl Sandburg

1

The Haw Branch Hauntings

Some thirty miles west of Richmond, Virginia, along U.S. Highway 360, lies a small town, not much more than a hamlet, called Amelia, Virginia. Ask anyone in Amelia, a mechanic at one of the two garages, the clerk at the only hotel or some passerby on the main street, how to get to Haw Branch. They are friendly folks and will gladly tell you. They know well of the old plantation. They know that strange things have been going on at Haw Branch for a long time.

The Haw Branch plantation dates back to pre-Revolutionary War days. There are no records of the area before 1735. But what chronicles now exist show that the manor house was built prior to that year. It could date back to the 1720's, and that part of it which was once an old inn may date back even earlier. To visit Haw Branch today is to enter a time machine and journey back to long, long ago.

The Haw Branch manor house is one of the most traditional homes in Virginia. It is situated on a low hill and set in a brick-paved depression resembling an ancient moat. The gleaming white three-and-a-half-story structure, with its towering chimneys, is surrounded by acres of rolling lawn and ancient magnolia, elm and tulip trees. Occasional gardens break the lawn's carpet effect. Outbuildings include the early kitchen (during the ante-bellum era, cooking was done in a building separate from the main house), a barn, a smokehouse and the old slave quarters—all restored. There is even a former private school on the grounds.

At one time, the whole plantation covered over fifteen thousand acres; and as many as five hundred slaves are believed to have worked there. The slaves were apparently well treated, for after the emancipation a number chose to stay on. There are two graveyards—one for family members and one for colored. Today, Haw Branch covers around two thousand acres.

If the grounds have the appearance of another era, then walking up the steps to the porch and entering the manor house may convince you that you are actually back in pre–Civil War days. Except for plumbing and electrical fixtures, the house is pure ante-bellum . . . with canopied beds, authentic wing-back chairs, handmade rugs, vintage utensils, a grandfather's clock and early family portraits. One of those portraits, the one hanging over the fireplace in the library, has a very bizarre history.

As you stand in the library at Haw Branch, something seems to draw your eyes toward the portrait of a beautiful young woman that hangs over the fireplace. The woman in the painting is Florence Wright, who lived in Duxbury, Massachusetts many years ago. The twenty-year-old woman's bright blue eyes sparkle below a crown of reddish brown hair. Her complexion has the appearance of living flesh. The green chair she sits in is upholstered in a shade of green even darker than the jade-colored vase on the table next to her. The soft pink rose in the vase looks real. The picture is contained in a huge hand-carved wooden frame.

2

Admiring the portrait of the beautiful young woman, a viewer would find it hard to believe that the painting is shrouded in mystery. Certainly I had no premonition that such is the case, as I looked up at the picture. Then the owners of Haw Branch told me the story:

Cary McConnaughey and his wife Gibson purchased Haw Branch in 1964. Mrs. McConnaughey hadn't seen the plantation since she was a child when her grandmother, Harriet Mason Jefferson, lived there. Her family had owned Haw Branch since before the American Revolution. It had been almost half a century since any of Gibson McConnaughey's family lived in the manor house.

When the McConnaugheys visited the plantation in 1964, the mansion was virtually in shambles from fifty years of neglect. After deciding that the building was restorable, they bought it and began an extensive restoration project. Then, on August 13, 1965, the McConnaugheys, their children and two dogs moved into the plantation house.

It was four years later that Gibson was given the portrait of Florence Wright by an elderly cousin. The girl in the painting was a distant relative connected by marriage. All the cousin knew was that when Florence's parents were alive, they had a summer home in Massachusetts, and that just before the painting was finished the young woman had suddenly died. The artist, whose name was forgotten, completed the work after the subject's death. During her short life Florence Wright never visited Haw Branch.

When the cousin gave the portrait to the McConnaugheys, she told them it was a beautifully colored pastel painting. After uncrating it and painstakingly cleaning the glass, they discovered what appeared to be a charcoal rendering of dirty white, gray and black rather than a colored painting. They could find no signature of the artist. The back was tightly sealed and they left it that way.

A few days after the portrait in its heavy frame was hung over the library fireplace, Gibson (Mrs. McConnaughey) was in the basement when she heard, coming from the library, the voices of several women engaged in conversation. Thinking it was probably some friends who had come to visit, she went upstairs, calling out, "I'm coming right up." She heard the voices until just before she reached the library. When she entered the room, there was no one there. Furthermore, she could find no one anywhere throughout the big house. And there were no cars in the parking area.

In February 1970, a few months later, Cary McConnaughey was seated in the library reading the Sunday paper. Glancing up, he noticed that the rose in the portrait was turning pink right before his eyes. He got up and walked over to the picture. He could see also that the girl's black hair was gradually beginning to lighten, and that her grayish skin was turning flesh-colored. In fact, nearly all of the blacks and grays in the portrait were taking on color. The changes continued slowly day by day. In the meantime, voices of young women talking and laughing were again heard coming from the library from time to time. But the origin of the sounds could never be found. With the passing of each day, the pastel hues became more obvious. It was only a matter of months before the colorless portrait was transformed into its present pastel brilliance.

A clairvoyant who lived in a neighboring county heard of the portrait that had changed color and called on the McConnaugheys. After studying the picture, he said that Florence Wright's spirit was permanently bound to the portrait because she died before it was completed, and that she had the power to remove the color from it when she was dissatisfied with where it hung. The spirit apparently accompanied the girl's portrait to Haw Branch.

Florence Wright liked Haw Branch. So, with help

from the spirits of two other young women, she restored the original color to her portrait. After the color had finally returned to the picture, the voices of the young women were not heard any more.

But there was more that would happen with the portrait of Florence Wright. In Gibson McConnaughey's own words, this is what occurred.

"One of our daughters and a visiting friend were sitting on the floor beneath the portrait as the family watched television about seven o'clock one summer night in 1972. The two girls decided to move over to the sofa, and less than one minute after they moved, the supports of the picture's heavy frame pulled loose. Then, as though a slow-motion camera was recording the scene, the portrait slowly slid down the wall until the bottom of the frame reached the mantel shelf where it crushed a row of porcelain antiques. The picture tipped forward slightly, slipped over the edge of the mantel and fell to the wide pine floorboards.

"As everyone in the room sat transfixed, staring in disbelief, there was a jarring bump and the tinkle of breaking glass that sent Smokey, our cat, yowling across the room in fright. The portrait had fallen face down on the exact spot where the girls had been sitting, making a dent in the floor. Broken glass was everywhere.

"Although the painting itself was undamaged, the big wooden frame was broken. Lifting it up, we found underneath what had been the tightly sealed backing of the frame, a brass plate that gave the girl's full name, her birth date in Duxbury, Massachusetts, and her date of death in the same place. Though we searched carefully for the artist's signature both on the front and the back of the painting, it could not be found."

As Gibson shifted her weight in the wing-back chair she was sitting in, she continued her story. "Next day, the frame was repaired, the portrait placed back in it and the glass replaced. The man who did the work searched as carefully as we had searched to find the artist's signature, but with no success.

"It was late in the day when we arrived back at Haw Branch with the portrait. The sun was low in the sky. As my husband and I lifted the picture from the back of the station wagon, I happened to tilt my end of the frame slightly upward. Suddenly, as though a red neon sign had been lit, the name, 'J. Wells Champney,' appeared. It had been signed in pencil on the apron of the dark mahogany table in the picture. Only under a certain angle of light could it be seen."

Cary McConnaughey now took over the story. "We learned that the beautiful woman in the portrait had been born into a wealthy family that owned several homes, including the one at Duxbury. Her parents commissioned Mr. Champney to paint the portrait. Then one day, when the painting was well along the way to completion, Florence Wright, twenty-four years old, was practicing at her piano. Suddenly she slumped over the keyboard. She died almost immediately from a massive stroke.

"The artist completed the portrait and added the partially opened rose to signify that his subject died an untimely death before the painting was completed."

"And do you know," added Gibson, "many people who come to Haw Branch and see Florence Wright's portrait say they can see a pink flush steal up her throat and spread to her cheeks!"

"Did you learn more about the artist?" I asked.

"He was killed when he fell down an elevator shaft in New York City," said Cary.

Although the mysterious incidents surrounding the portrait of Florence Wright are beyond the bounds of ordinary knowledge, they were not terrifying per se. But horror and fright have prevailed at Haw Branch.

Early in the pre-dawn darkness of November 23, 1965, the entire McConnaughey family was awakened by a woman's blood-curdling scream that seemed to come from upstairs. Rushing up the steps from their first-floor bedroom, Gibson and Cary found their children gathered at the foot of the staircase that leads from the second floor to the attic. The children had decided that the scream originated in the attic. Porkchop and Blackie, the family's two dogs, were shaking with terror. No one volunteered to check the attic until well into the daylight hours, when nothing amiss was found there. This incident occurred three months after the McConnaugheys moved into Haw Branch, and it was the first inkling they had that something might be seriously wrong in the manor.

In February, a few months later, all six members of the McConnaughey family were sitting in the library watching television one night when they heard a jolting thud from outdoors that shook the house. "It sounded as though a very heavy solid object such as a safe had fallen from a great height and landed on the bricks of the moat that surrounds the house," said Gibson McConnaughey. "We rushed outside with flashlights, expecting to find something lying there. But nothing unusual was found."

The sound of a heavy object falling into the moat has been heard both at regular and irregular intervals ever since. On some occasions, it occurs during daylight hours.

Investigation by the McConnaugheys has revealed that previous residents also experienced the same weird happenings. (To our knowledge the last thumping occurred several weeks before Nancy and I visited Haw Branch in July 1978.)

On May 23, 1966, six months to the day since the McConnaugheys heard the scream in the night, a woman's anguished scream again echoed through the halls of Haw Branch. And, as in the previous incident, no source for the sound could be located.

Six months later, on November 23, the terrifying shriek of a woman's voice again resounded through

Haw Branch just before dawn. This time Porkchop jumped into an open chest and Blackie buried himself under a blanket on the bed.

Then, shortly before dawn on May 23, 1967, exactly six months to the day since the last shrieking occurrence, the woman's scream from the attic was heard once more.

During the summer of 1967, Gibson and her husband were sitting up late one night reading. Shortly after one, Cary went to bed. Gibson stopped off in the kitchen to get a glass of milk. Except for an upstairs light the house was dark. As Gibson opened the refrigerator door and the inside light dimly lit the hall between the kitchen and the library, she happened to glance into the hall where something caught her eye: "I could plainly see the silhouette of a slim girl in a floor-length dress with a full skirt. It was not the wide fullness of a hoop-skirt, but one from an earlier period. I could see no features but she was not transparent, just a white silhouette. I saw her for perhaps ten seconds. In the next instant she was gone. There was no gradual fading away; she simply disappeared from one instant to the next.

"I rushed to our bedroom and told my husband what I had seen. He laughed so hard that I didn't mention it to anyone else."

Several days later, one of the McConnaughey daughters approached her mother with the report of another harrowing visitation. When the daughter told her story, she knew absolutely nothing of what her mother had seen several nights previously.

The daughter began talking: "Blackie's barking on the front porch kept me awake last night, so I went downstairs and let her in. She scampered right past me and into the drawing room. When I looked into the drawing room, Blackie was sitting there wagging her tail and looking up at a lady in white who was standing in front of the fireplace. Before I could say

8

anything the lady disappeared right in front of my eyes."

Gibson McConnaughey later found out that previous residents of Haw Branch had also seen "The Lady in White." At a family reunion the subject was brought up, and an older relative mentioned the fact that their great grandmother, Harriet B. Mason, had told of having seen the White Lady. She had even been awakened out of a sound sleep by a touch from the apparition.

There are times at Haw Branch when, instead of seeing the apparition of "The Lady in White," footsteps are heard descending from the attic to the second floor. Immediate investigations have disclosed only empty stairways.

On other occasions, lights have gone on by themselves when the names of certain ancestors who lived on the plantation in centuries past were mentioned. Sometimes lights that are already on go off for the same reason.

And there have been instances when the aroma of oranges being peeled, or roses, have permeated parts of the house, when actually no roses or oranges were on the premises.

The odor of fresh oranges was first noticed in November 1967. At the time only canned, frozen orange juice was in the house and all of the cans were unopened. Later that same week the McConnaughey family was sitting around the dinner table discussing the aromas. Gibson mentioned the name of her great grandmother, Harriet Mason, and immediately two bulbs in the electric chandelier over the dining room table grew extremely brilliant, almost like photo flashlights, and then they went out.

A week later, on November 23, realizing that it was again that time of the year for the mysterious woman's pre-dawn scream to be heard, the family made preparations for the coming event with several flashlights and a tape recorder. From midnight to dawn, they took turns staying awake. The two dogs and the cat behaved very nervously, but the scream was not heard that night.

On May 23, 1968, the McConnaugheys again waited, this time with flashlights and a tape recorder. While waiting for the scream, the entire family heard something walking across the yard with heavy footsteps. At the same time an eerie screeching wail penetrated the night.

"When the heavy footsteps began," Gibson said, "my husband and I attempted to step quietly out onto the porch to see what it was. We heard something running heavily, and in a matter of only several seconds, heard the call come from beyond the barn.

"Next morning our son and one daughter reported that they saw a giant bird standing in the yard in the moonlight under their windows. It was standing there with its wings spread out, appearing to have a wingspan of over six feet."

Although the woman's screams were never heard again, the screech of the giant bird was heard on a number of occasions, but the bird itself hasn't been seen since. The screeches were always heard only on the twenty-third of May or November. However, at the time of this writing, it's been several years since the family has heard the screech of the giant night bird.

Ever since the McConnaugheys moved into Haw Branch, a number of untraceable noises have been heard in the manor house and on the surrounding grounds.

One May night in 1972, McConnaughey's son and some young friends were sleeping in the old slave quarters building. Throughout the night they kept hearing cowbells coming from the pasture. Yet, each time they looked out, there would be nothing there. Sometimes the sound of the cowbell would actually seem to encircle the building, but still their flashlights showed only an empty pasture. At that time there were no cows at Haw Branch Plantation.

There was also an occasion when what looked like a man carrying a lighted kerosene lantern emerged from the barn. The light was bobbing as it neared the house. As it passed the porch, there was no man to be seen—only the moving lantern. It rounded the corner of the house and vanished.

Not only are the sounds of a heavy object falling into the moat still heard at Haw Branch, but so are other noises—especially from the attic. Ever since the family moved into the old mansion, the children, who sleep upstairs, have told of hearing noises like furniture being moved around in the attic above their rooms. Even when the elder McConnaugheys slept upstairs, they, too, could hear the noise that sounded like furniture being dragged across the attic floor. Subsequent investigations revealed that all of the dust-covered furniture stored in the attic was unmoved. There were no traces of small animals or birds that might possibly have gotten inside the house.

An old rocking chair stored in the same attic is sometimes heard to rock in the night. Yet the chair is broken and would support no one.

At other times, a strange-humming sound is heard in the basement. Once Mrs. McConnaughey wrote down the tune: C - C - B Flat - B Flat - C - C - E Flat, C - C - B Flat - B Flat - A Flat. A musician friend who listened to the melody said it closely resembled an old English folk tune.

Is the answer to the Haw Branch mystery contained in the attic of the house? Possibly, but it's also conceivable that the answer lies in the basement. For down below is a sealed room—a chamber measuring approximately four by six feet and completely closed off by brick and masonry. It is a room that seems to hold some strange fascination for the McConnaughey dogs and cat.

11

A woman's terrifying scream just before dawn; a kerosene lantern floating across the yard; cowbells from phantom cows; the sound of moving furniture from furniture that isn't moved; the sound of a very heavy object falling, after which no object can be found; footsteps in the night; the ghostly woman in white; a tragically bizarre portrait; dogs terrified by something unseen; a giant man-sized bird with a blood-curdling screech—what horrible trauma could have occurred at Haw Branch in years past to bring these unexplainable things about? What deep, dark secret does the house hold—a house whose previous owner died suddenly just a few hours after signing over the deed . . . ?

This vile, heinous, unknown devil,
torturer of human flesh, that preyed
upon the fears of people like
a ravenous vulture, spared her not . . .
Richard Williams Bell

2

The Bell Witch—The Witch That Is Really A Ghost

The Red River, a tributary of the Cumberland River, runs through a gulley next to Bill Eden's land in north-central Tennessee, about halfway up the embankment where the mysterious Bell Witch Cave is located. It is a deep cave and one that is permeated with the unknown. Although the story of the Bell Witch is considered by some to be no more than a legend, many folks in Robertson County and elsewhere in Tennessee not only believe that the Bell Witch did exist, but that she, or it, still roams, haunts and terrorizes the countryside. On occasion, down through the years, it has taken the form of a bird, a rabbit and even a dog.

In the beginning of the last century, north-central Tennessee was, as it is today, primarily agricultural. The early farmers raised cotton, flax, sheep and produce.

John Bell, his wife Lucy, together with their children, slaves and livestock, settled near Adams Station, as Adams, Tennessee, was called in 1804. Bell bought an existing farmhouse with a thousand acres of land along the banks of the Red River.

13

Within half a decade, John Bell's family became one of the wealthiest and most respected in the tiny Baptist Bible-belt town. And John himself was considered one of the staunchest pillars of the community. Lucy bore him eight children.

Richard Powell, the local schoolmaster, taught the Bell children. He took a special liking to the Bell's oldest daughter Betsy. However, Betsy had a second suitor—young Joshua Gardner. It was during this period that the Bell Witch entered the lives of the John Bell family.

The first sighting occurred when John Bell saw a strange-looking dog prancing between some cornstalks. He shot at the creature, but when he went to see what he'd hit, there was nothing there.

The second sighting was shortly thereafter, when John and two of his boys spotted a bird—larger than a turkey, but unlike any other bird they'd ever seen—perched in an oak tree. John fired, and the bird appeared to fall to the ground. But when the two boys reached the site, they found no trace of the bird.

One afternoon a few weeks later, Betsy saw a girl about her own age dressed in green and sitting in a swing attached to the same oak tree. When Betsy ran toward the tree, the girl in the swing vanished.

Dean, one of the Bell slaves, reported a large black snarling dog that would disappear when he approached it with a stick.

During the time of these sightings neither the Bell family nor anyone else was aware of the existence of the Bell Witch. Their neighbor Alex Gunn suggested that they had "active imaginations."

But soon, disturbances began occurring at the Bell house. There were knockings on the door when no one was there. Windows rattled on windless nights. This was a tame beginning, however, compared to what was yet to come.

Week after week, an invisible rat gnawed savagely on bed posts. An unseen dog clawed at the floor.

There were sounds of fighting dogs chained together. These noises grew more terrifying with the passing of each week. They spread from room to room. When members of the family woke up and searched for the source, the noises stopped.

There were now sounds of choking and gurgling. New sounds were heard—chains dragging across the floors and furniture being moved about. The covers were ripped from beds while they were being slept in. If an awakened sleeper attempted to struggle with the force removing the bedding, an invisible hand would slap his or her face, leaving it red and sore. Some of the children even had their hair violently pulled. Daughter Betsy ran screaming in horror from her room on numerous occasions, but could never explain what led to the action.

Her two suitors, young Joshua Gardner and the old schoolmaster Richard Powell, were now actively seeking Betsy's hand. Betsy was inclined to choose the man nearer her own age as her beau. And it seemed that whenever Betsy "entertained" Joshua, the Witch would make the young blue-eyed daughter of John Bell the victim of that night's visitation.

Betsy was finally moved to the homes of friends and neighbors in an attempt to get her away from the cruelty of the Witch. But there was no escape, for the spirit, or whatever it was, followed her, then treating her even more brutally. She suffered fainting spells, had the breath sucked out of her body and felt sensations that she was being smothered. There was a feeling that her body was being stuck with pins and needles. On one occasion, the Witch even caused Betsy to appear to vomit a mouthful of pins and needles.

John Bell and some friends formed a committee to investigate the evil phenomenon that had taken over his house. From all over Tennessee and Kentucky came exorcists, dewitchers, and other expellers of evil spirits—all hoping to eliminate the Bell Witch. Their efforts were all in vain—almost. James Johnson, a neighbor, finally established communication with the terror that had been plaguing the Bells.

After listening to various noises emanating from the entity, such as the smacking of lips, gulping and the hissing of breath being sucked through teeth, Johnson determined that the thing had an intelligence. When he announced this contention publicly, the attacks on Betsy temporarily ceased. Then the assaults on her intensified. And now they were even worse than before.

Richard, one of John Bell's sons, wrote: "This vile, heinous, unknown devil, torturer of human flesh, that preyed upon the fears of people like a ravenous vulture, spared her not, but rather chose her as a shining mark for or exhibition of its wicked stratagem and devilish tortures. And never did it cease to practice upon her fears, insult her modesty, stick pins in her body, pinching and bruising her flesh, slapping her cheeks, disheveling and untangling her hair, tormenting her in many ways until she surrendered that most cherished hope which animates every young heart."

The Bell Witch infamy spread far and wide, and almost every night the Bell house was packed with persons—all attempting to communicate with it.

At first it knocked in response to their attempts. Then it began to whistle when addressed. Soon the whistling developed into a sort of whisper that eventually became more articulate. The talking occurred day or night in both lighted and dark rooms.

At first Betsy herself was accused by some skeptics of being a ventriloquist. This imputation was challenged and disproved when a doctor placed his hand over Betsy's mouth while the Witch's voice spewed forth a volley of words.

Soon the Witch's talking became both louder and clearer. When asked to explain itself, it replied, "I am a spirit from everywhere, Heaven, Hell, the Earth. I am in the air, in houses, any place at any time. I've been created millions of years. That is all I will tell you."

Then one night it said, "I am determined to haunt and torment old Jack [John] Bell as long as he lives." And the Bell Witch thus began tormenting John Bell. John had been suffering from a facial twitch ever since the Witch's presence first became known, but had never associated it with the visitations.

As the attacks on Betsy diminished, they increased on her father. Discussing the situation with a friend, Mahala Darden, he said, "All of a sudden, my tongue became strangely affected. Something that felt like a fungus growth came on both sides, pressing against my jaws, filling my mouth so that I could not eat or talk."

The Witch's afflictions on John Bell intensified. There were times when his tongue swelled up to the extent that his entire face became misshapen. These spells lasted as long as two or three days. Then he would be up and about his business once again. But as time passed, the Witch grew angrier and more virulent and blasted John Bell with curses and heinous threats. Yet his wife Lucy was treated tenderly and with loving respect.

During one of John's more severe attacks, which lasted eight days, "The Witch cursed and raved like a maniac for those days and ceased not troubling him."

There were times when George Hapson, the family doctor, would enter John's room and set his bag on the floor. Within a few minutes there'd be the sound of breaking glass as if every pill and medicine bottle in the kit had broken. Yet, when the doctor would rush over and look inside the bag, he would find nothing disturbed.

John was over that eight-day siege no more than a week when the Witch changed its tactics. John and his son Richard were walking down the road to the hog pen about three hundred yards from the house. John was totally recovered from his last attack and feeling quite strong. About halfway to the pen, the Witch struck again.

The incident is best told in the words of Richard Williams Bell. "We had not gone far before one of his shoes was jerked off. I replaced it on his foot, drawing the strings tight, tying a double hard knot.

"After going a few steps farther, the other shoe flew off in the same manner, which was replaced and tied as in the case of the first. In no way that I could tie them, would they hold, notwithstanding his shoes fitted close and were a little hard to put on, and we were walking over a smooth, dry road.

"After much delay and worry, we reached the place and tended the hogs, and we started back for the house. We had not gone many steps before his shoes commenced jerking off as before, and presently he complained of a blow on his face, which felt like an open hand, that almost stunned him, and he sat down on a log that lay by the roadside.

"Then his face commenced jerking with fearful contortions, soon his whole body, and then his shoes would fly off as fast as I could put them on.

"The situation was trying and made me shudder. I was terrified by the spectacle of the contortions that seized Father, as if to convert him into a very demon to swallow me up.

"Having finished tying Father's shoes, I raised myself up to hear the reviling sound of derisive songs piercing the air with terrorizing force. As the demonic shrieks died away in triumphant rejoicing, the spell passed off, and I saw the tears chasing down Father's yet quivering cheeks."

Richard then went on reporting his father's words after the attack: "Oh, my son, my son, not long will you have a father to wait on so patiently. I cannot much longer survive the persecutions of this terrible thing. It is killing me by slow tortures, and I feel the end is nigh."

On recovering his senses, John Bell returned to the

house feeling calm and collected. But he was never to leave the homestead alive. For no sooner had he entered the house than he immediately took to his bed. His strength gradually declined. The fact that the Witch continued its deviltry hastened the declination.

On the morning of December 19, 1820, John Bell was found to be lying in an unnatural position and in a complete stupor. All attempts to awaken him proved fruitless. As John, Jr., went to the cupboard for his father's medicine, his brother Drew went to Port Royal to get Dr. Hapson.

But instead of finding his father's medicine in the cabinet, John, Jr., discovered a vial of dark-colored liquid. Neighbors James Johnson, Alex Gunn and Frank Miles arrived. They were all still speculating on the contents of the vial as Dr. Hapson entered.

As the doctor bent over the unconscious form on the bed, the voice of the Witch broke out: "It's useless for you to try to relieve old Jack. I have got him this time. He will never get up from that bed again."

One of the neighbors asked, "What is this vial?"

The Witch's voice said: "I put it there and gave old Jack a big dose out of it last night while he was asleep, which fixed him." No other information could be found about the vial or its contents. The doctor said it was not any medicine that he had brought to the house. Someone suggested that the medicine be tested on something. Alex Gunn picked up a cat and John, Jr., placed a drop of the vial's contents on the feline's tongue.

The cat swirled in circles for several seconds, rolled over on its back and died. John Bell lay all that day and night in a semi-coma from which he could not be aroused. Dr. Hapson said that John Bell's breath smelled similar to the contents of the vial. Without taking any further samples of the vial for chemical evaluation, Dr. Hapson threw it into the fire. Like an explosion, a sudden blue flame shot up the chimney.

During the night, the Witch was heard in John Bell's room partaking in jubilation and at the same time deriding the dying man. By morning, John Bell was dead. Nothing more was heard from the Witch until the day of the funeral.

It was a cold, bright December day. There were more persons gathered at John Bell's graveside than had ever been reported at a Tennessee funeral before. After the service was finished, the grave diggers commenced shoveling the dirt back into John Bell's last resting place.

Then, as the crowd began to disperse, their low-voiced conversation was suddenly drowned out by a loud, shrill voice. It was the Bell Witch singing, over and over, "Row Me Up Some Brandy O."

Following the death of John Bell, Sr., the blasphemous fury of the Witch diminished, and in the spring of 1821, it took leave of the Bell family with the promise that it would return in seven years.

By this time young Betsy had grown into a shapely blue-eyed woman with waist-length blonde hair. She had accepted an engagement ring from Joshua Gardner, and plans for their wedding were being made. The lovers were left in a pleasant reverie over the fact that the Witch had left. But the wedding between the young lovers was not to be.

The couple were haunted by the shrill, screeching voice of the Witch pleading: "Please, Betsy Bell, don't have Joshua Gardner." The entreaty was repeated over and over, and with each repetition it became more like a warning.

Fearing that if the wedding were to take place, the destiny of both Joshua and herself would be not unlike that of her late agonized father, Betsy grew apprehensive and the wedding was called off.

Richard Powell, the schoolmaster, renewed his courting of Betsy, and they were eventually betrothed. Powell died seventeen years later and Betsy remained a widow until her death in 1890 at the age of eighty-six.

Joshua Gardner moved to western Tennessee where he lived a prosperous life and died at the age of eighty-four.

The Bell Witch remained dormant for seven years after destroying Betsy and Joshua's marriage plans. But in 1828, it returned as promised. Mrs. Bell and two of her sons, Joel and Richard, were the only occupants of the old homestead, the other children having gone off on their own. The family agreed to totally ignore the tapping and scraping noises, along with other poltergeistic activities that were taking place. The Witch departed after two weeks and visited the home of John, Jr. And there, she promised to return again "in one hundred years and seven."

There were numerous paranormal confrontations in Robertson County during the time the Bell Witch promised to remain absent. Some were attributed to the Witch, but almost all could just as well have been due to the activities of other entities. Many stories of the Witch surfaced during those years—some documented and others discounted.

John Bell, Jr., disclosed a conversation that he had with the Witch before his father died. Young Bell's statement was the first hint of the Witch's ability as a prophet. The Witch's predictions would make many of those modern psychics whose forecasts appear in some national tabloid papers look pretty mediocre.

Among the things prophesied by the Bell Witch were the coming of the War between the States, the end of slavery in the United States, the United States becoming a world power and World Wars I and II. All came true as predicted. The Witch dated World War II to within four years of when it actually took place.

The Witch made another prediction which has yet to happen. That was the total destruction of our civilization. This foretelling was worded to give the hint of a nuclear holocaust, for there was the mention of rapidly increasing heat followed by a horrendous explosion. The time for the fulfillment of this last prophecy was not given.

Although the Bell Witch accurately forecast many great changes to come in American history, its foretold return in one hundred and seven years, or 1935, apparently didn't take place, for there are no available reports of anything having happened to verify the return.

However, Susy Smith, in her book *Ghosts Around the House*, presents information that could well indicate that certain descendants of John Bell are still falling under the curse of the Bell Witch—even more horribly than did their ancestor.

Smith tells of an interview she had with Robert Borden Adam, son of Ann Bell Adam. Adam's mother was the daughter of John Elijah Bell II of Tennessee. During the interview, which took place in 1969, Adam told about how, in 1968, he was sent home on emergency leave from Navy boot camp in San Diego after his two sisters and father burned to death in the family home. Although fire investigators did not rule out arson, the twenty-one-year-old sailor felt that the fire was set—by the Bell Witch.

Several months later, his mother, Ann Bell Adam, fatally succumbed after consuming eighty-seven sleeping pills.

Robert also told Ms. Smith that his great grandfather, John Elijah Bell I, came to a sudden and violent death in Memphis when struck by a speeding ambulance.

Robert's Grandmother Bell, John Elijah II's widow, was afflicted in 1969 by a malady not unlike that which plagued the original John Bell . . . a mysterious nerve ailment accompanied by a stiffness of the throat and mouth that prevented her from talking.

Is it possible that the tragedies that overtook John Bell's descendants in recent years may have been coincidental? The fire could have been an explainable tragedy. The suicide of Ann Bell Adam might have resulted from despondency over the loss of her husband and daughters. Many people have died as John Elijah Bell I did, after being run over by a speeding vehicle. Are there medical records of the first John Bell's death to compare with the demise of Robert's grandmother? No, it's not impossible to explain these related misfortunes as a series of explainable happenings totally unattributable to the Bell Witch. But, on the other hand, what if the Bell Witch has come back?

The Bell Witch has returned. It has remanifested itself on Bill Eden's farm which was once land belonging to John Bell. Eden, his family and even visitors to the farm have encountered the Bell Witch. As of this writing, the Witch stalks Bill Eden's land.

What was once, in the early 1800's, the main highway leading down from the north to Nashville is now a two-rut dirt road less than one-hundred and fifty yards long, running between Bill Eden's house and his barn. In recent years, ghostly encounters with the Bell Witch have been quite prevalent on this road and in the surrounding countryside.

When Nancy and I first called at the Eden house, Mrs. Eden answered the door. After a cordial exchange of greetings she pointed down the ancient road and said, "You'll find Bill over there in the barn."

The sensation one gets walking along the road to the barn is quite eerie. It is a sort of nostalgic feeling. Your thoughts seem to be divided between the wagons and coaches that once traveled into history along the same ground more than a century and a half ago, and speculations on where the Bell Witch is now.

"The Witch is here, all right," said Bill Eden. "She's all around here."

When I first laid eyes on this man, as he bent over to repair a plow blade, I couldn't help but think

23

that he looked more like a typical mid-American farmer than any person I'd ever seen. Neither a hick nor a redneck type, he more or less reminded me of the movie star Henry Fonda in build and expression. He is one of those ageless-looking individuals who could have been anywhere between forty-five and sixty-five—maybe older or maybe younger. His features are those of an outdoor man who has spent most of his life toiling against the elements.

Bill Eden belongs to a vanishing breed, a breed that made America the nation it is today. His kind is gradually being pushed off the stage by absentee farmers, corporations, tenant farmers, gentlemen farmers and land developers.

It is said that every American should see San Francisco before he dies. Well, every American should also visit a real family-owned and family-worked American farm before he dies. But if he or she also has a fear of enigmas that are beyond the bounds of the ordinary and shrouded in the unknown, then it might be best not to stop off at the Bill Eden place—especially the area near the Bell Witch's Cave.

"They call me William, they call me W.M., they call me Bill, they call me Judd and they call me 'the Bell Witch man,' " is the way Bill Eden introduced himself to us.

Adjusting my tape recorder, I asked Bill, "Do you believe the Bell Witch still exists?"

He straightened up from the work he was doing and answered, "Yes, sir!"

"Why?"

"Because there are too many things which happen here that you can't explain," he replied, looking back down at his work.

"Tell me about some."

Bill laid aside a crescent wrench that he was working with and stood up. "I was coming from this milk barn here on the way to the house one night when something took hold of my arm. I thought it was one of my boys hidin' beside the road trying to scare me. I lit my cigarette lighter and there was nobody on the road but me. I couldn't hear no sound and couldn't see nothing. There wasn't anything there that you could see at all.

"Also, we had footsteps come through our new house . . . We tore the old house down that stood where our new house is standing now. We hear knocking at the door as well, or walking down the hall. A few weeks ago, my wife was fixin' dinner and she heard someone in the basement like they were draggin' an old straight-backed chair around. So she went down there twice and still she couldn't find anything.

"And those cabinet doors in the kitchen, sometimes we'll be sittin' there eatin' and the doors are partially open. Suddenly, like someone came along and hit them with their hand, they'll slam shut. Or sometimes they'll be closed and, bloop, one of them'll fly open."

Ignoring the rain clouds that were stealthily sneaking up on us, I continued with my questioning. "Did you ever actually see anything?"

"Back in January, when all of that snow and ice was on the ground, well, one mornin' about two o'clock, something woke me up knockin' on the front door. I got up—and I had to go into the living room to get to the front door—and when I got there instead of going to the door I just raised the curtains so I could see out, but there wasn't anybody there.

"So I went back to my bedroom, and instead of going to bed I went into the bathroom and there I lit myself up a cigar and sat on the commode 'n' smoked. In a few minutes, the knock came again and knocked about three times, so I sneaked back in there to the living room to look. There was someone, looked like a person, walkin' out my front walkway that appeared to have on a long black coat pulled up high around its ears and was almost draggin' on the ground. But, now, I couldn't tell whether it was a man or a woman. I couldn't tell. So when it got to the end of my walk, it turned and went down the hill. I saw that there wasn't any car out there, and I kept wondering where the car was. It went behind a big tree but didn't come out from the other side. So I called my wife and woke her up. She came to the living room and said, 'What in the world are you doing in here?'

"I said, 'Come in here and watch behind this tree till I get my clothes on and fetch my gun.' I thought it was someone trying to break in. That's what I thought it was.

"So I got dressed and went down through the basement with my shotgun and my light and sneaked a way around and came all the way behind it. And I kept peeping and looking and walked clear around that tree. I looked down for the tracks in the snow. But there was only my tracks. And I looked over the walkway, and there wasn't a single track on my walkway. And so, it's such things that make me believe in ghosts."

Reaching down, Bill picked up a flat file and went back to work on the plow blade as he talked. "One Sunday, there was this girl who came up to visit from Nashville. We all went down by the river to fish while she stayed up here.

"Well, when we came back up here, she said she walked around to the front of my house on that hill and she was just sittin' there, you know, lookin' around for rocks and just makin' herself at home, and there was a girl that walked up to her. Said she was blonde-headed, sort of blondish-lookin', had blue eyes and her hair hung down to her waist. And she thought she just walked up there where she was at, and she said she looked back around to say something to her, and she was gone."

I glanced up to see how close the rain clouds were getting and then asked, "What kind of clothes did she have on?"

"Said she was dressed in a long black skirt and a white blouse."

I glanced at Nancy and knew she was thinking the same thing I was—the apparition matched the description of Betsy Bell as a young woman. Could Betsy's spirit be haunting the land that once belonged to her father—or could the Bell Witch have materialized in Betsy's likeness?

Bill continued talking. "Some lady came here to go to the cave. So we started off down to the cave, about twelve or fifteen of us. All at once this lady, she just sat down in the path. One of the people who was with her asked what she was doing sitting down in the path. She answered, 'I'm not sitting here. Something lit on my back just like a heavy weight— like a ton of lead and just pressed me into the ground. I can't get up.' So they got ahold of her arms and they helped her up and got her back up the hill to the car."

A light drizzle had begun to fall, but Bill kept working on the plow blade so I kept the interview going. "Bill, has anything ever happened inside the Bell Witch Cave?"

"Oh, yeah" was his reply. "You can hear footsteps in there at times. And I only saw one thing. Lots of people come out here expecting to see a ghost or a witch or whatever you want to call it. I just call it a spirit, and I only saw one thing and it looked like a person with its back turned to you. Looked like it was built out of real white-looking heavy fog or snow, or something real solid white. But you couldn't see through it. It had the complete figure of a person till it got down to about its ankles. It wasn't touchin' the floor at all. It was just drifting —bouncin' along. There was five of us there at the time."

"Did anyone try to catch whatever it is that's being seen around here?"

As we moved under the eave of the barn to get

out of the rain, Bill said, "An old man and his sister used to live in the old house here before I tore it down. He said there was a big tree that stood out there, and there was a big light, looked like an old oil lamp, that used to set up in that tree and burn at night back when he was a boy. He said, 'One night Pappy said he was goin' to take his old rifle and shoot that light. So he shot it. And, of course, we all ran down there to see what Pappy killed. Got down there an' there wasn't anything at all to see.' His name was Cope and he was about eighty at the time he told me that story."

"Mr. Eden," asked Nancy, "did anything ever happen to you in the daylight?"

Wiping his brow, Bill turned to her and said, "Lots of times I'll be out here in the fields workin' an' what sounds like a woman's voice will speak up and holler my name, 'Bill, Bill, hey, Bill.' An' I'll turn around an' look but I can't find nobody at all. An' my wife has heard her name called several times; her name is Frances. It'll say, 'Frances,' just like that!

"'Bout two years ago, she was in the kitchen fixin' lunch and it sounded like someone came through the front door and came in with a chain draggin'. They came in and dragged it all the way through the livin' room, into the dinin' room and right into the kitchen to where she was standing by her cook stove, just like they were draggin' a log chain and then just split off. But she couldn't see a thing. And she heard a woman's voice scream out two or three different times there in the kitchen. Just a loud, shrill scream.

"But I've also heard that same scream in the cave. But I could never catch up with it enough to see. I could never see it."

"Did it seem to lead you on into the cave or something?" I asked.

"Yeah, uh huh. I followed it plumb back as far as I could. It just stayed ahead of me enough that I couldn't catch up with it. An' about every two seconds it'd scream like a woman would scream—like she was in misery of some sort. But I could never catch up with her enough to see her."

I changed the tape recorder to my other hand and asked, "Did you ever get a medium or spiritualist here to try to communicate with the spirit?"

"No, no, I haven't. They did the year before I bought the place. They tried it, but they had such a huge crowd that they couldn't quiet 'em down enough to try anything. There was over four thousand people here that night. The crowd just made so much noise, they couldn't communicate with it at all."

"Tell me, Mr. Eden," said Nancy, "are there any Bells still living around here?"

"There's one, a friend of mine. His mother—she had inherited all this bunch of old china dishes, you know, and had 'em in a cabinet. She hadn't used 'em in forty or fifty years. She lived just two houses down the street from her son. And so, one morning, it sounded like every dish in those cabinets fell out onto the floor and broke all to pieces. She thought somebody broke into the house on her. She was an old lady, so she called her son and told him to get up there quick ''cause there's someone in the dining room breaking all my dishes.' So he grabbed his pistol and took off down the street. When he got in the house, every dish that was up in those cabinets was layin' all over the floor. And there wasn't even a cracked dish in the whole bunch."

"How long ago was that?" I asked.

"That happened about three years ago—I think in 1975."

What Bill had just said reminded me of the incidents of Dr. Hapson, who heard the sounds of breaking glass in his medical bag while he was treating John Bell in 1820.

Nancy asked if there were any of the Bell family's old houses still standing. Bill reached down and with a piece of rag wiped dry the plow blade that he was working on. He said, "I lived with some of the Bells over here. The house would fill up with smoke and run their company off, you know, things like that. They all got scared and moved away from the place —said they couldn't live there any more.

"So I lived on in there. All I ever had happen, sounded like a team of horses or mules running across the front porch. It had a wooden floor. But you could jump up and run outside and look all you wanted to and there'd be nothing to see. It happened many times. So I finally poured a concrete porch. But that didn't help.

"And a funny thing, that old house, right today, the lady that lives across the road, she told me last summer the lights upstairs still light up any time of the day or night and there hasn't been an electric line goin' to the house for years. And she says those lights still come on upstairs."

As Nancy and I followed a winding wooded trail down the river embankment to the cave, the rain began to fall harder making the path rather slippery. Over the sound of the rain we could hear the roar of the Red River below. It had swollen over its banks as the result of a torrential rain that had fallen the night before.

Within a few minutes we would hear yet another roar even louder than that of the raging river. It came from the Bell Witch Cave.

Fate did not intend to let us enter the Bell Cave that day. A two-feet-deep torrent of water was rushing out of the mouth of the cave. Far back in its inner reaches, storm water was draining into the grotto.

We contemplated wading on into the cave anyway. But if there was this much water pouring out of the cavern after only a drizzle, how much more would there be now that the rain was intensifying?

"No," I said to Nancy. "It's too dangerous to go in there now. A ghost is one thing. But Mother

Nature can be worse, and if you combine them . . . well, no way."

We trudged back up the hill, and it was none too soon. There was a crash of thunder and then it seemed as if the entire sky opened up.

So I didn't get to go very far into the Bell Witch Cave. But by the time you read this, I will have. For something, I can't explain what, keeps beckoning me back to that cave to find out why the Bell Witch man said, "I just don't go back into the cave too far by myself."

3

The
Winchester Mystery House
—The House
That Fear Built

Leonard and Sarah L. Pardee, of New Haven, Connecticut, announced the birth of their daughter, Sarah, in September 1839. As young Sarah reached maturity, she became the belle of the town. Her accomplishments at the piano and organ made her the hit of old New Haven's social events. Before her eighteenth birthday she could speak fluently in four languages besides English. She was a petite young woman—very petite, only four feet ten inches tall. But what she lacked in size she made up for in beauty and personality.

Another prominent nineteenth-century New Havenite was a man named Oliver Winchester. Winchester, a shirt manufacturer, was a shrewd businessman. In 1857, he took over the assets of a firm making the Volcanic Repeater, a gun that used a lever mechanism to load bullets into the breech.

In 1860, Oliver's company developed the Henry rifle, which had a tubular magazine under the barrel. The Henry rifle could average one shot every three seconds, thus making it the first true repeater rifle. It was a favorite among Civil War troops.

As the money poured in and his fortune soared, Oliver Winchester reorganized his company, renaming it the Winchester Repeating Arms Company. The new firm produced the famous Winchester rifles—weapons that were a vast improvement on the Henry rifle. Cartridges were fed into the magazine through a small gate near the breech. The rifle was an immediate success not only because of its fast action, but also because its brass center-fire bullets could also be used in a number of Colt revolvers. Therefore, only one supply of ammo was needed for both the pistol and the rifle.

Every so often, the company would turn out a special rifle termed a one-in-a-hundred, or one-in-a-thousand. Today, these special arms are worth a small fortune among gun collectors.

On September 30, 1862, during the height of the Civil War when the Henry rifle was accounting for scores of fallen soldiers each day, William Wirt Winchester, Oliver Winchester's son, and Sarah Pardee were married in an elaborate ceremony.

Four years later, on July 15, 1866, Sarah Pardee Winchester gave birth to a daughter, Annie Pardee. A week later, the first tragedy in the life of Sarah struck. The infant came down with marasmus, a disease of children in which the body wastes away, and died on July 24, 1866. Sarah was so grief-stricken over the loss of her child that it was nearly fifteen years before she returned to her normal self.

Then a new tragedy shattered Sarah Winchester's life. Her husband, heir to the fortune derived from "the gun that won the West," died of pulmonary tuberculosis on March 7, 1881. As a result of her husband's death, Sarah Winchester inherited twenty million dollars, 48.8 percent of the Winchester

Repeating Arms Company and an income of one thousand dollars a day, which was tax free until 1913. Still the distraught widow grieved, not only for her late husband but anew for the child she had lost fifteen years earlier. Her health began deteriorating.

Doctors and friends tried unsuccessfully to get her to leave New England and seek a milder climate. But her grief was too deep-seated to permit her to leave the area where her husband and daughter were buried.

Soon, the Winchester rifle began to acquire a new reputation as the gun that killed more Indians, more game and more American troops than any other gun in American history. One day a friend suggested that Sarah should visit a medium on the possibility that a clairvoyant might alleviate some of her grief.

Sarah Winchester traveled to Boston to consult a spiritualistic medium. The seeress, who was highly respected among the occult community, said to Sarah, "There is a curse on your life. It is the same curse that took your child and husband. It will soon take you. It is a curse that has resulted from the terrible weapon that the Winchester family created. Thousands and thousands of persons, both whites and Indians, have fallen before that blasphemous instrument of death. Their spirits will drive you to your grave, too."

The sobbing widow buried her head in her hands and asked, "Tell me, what can I do to stop the spirits? I'll do anything."

"People have told you to go far away from here —far away to start a new life. Do so. Then build a house not only for yourself but also for the spirits of those who have fallen before that terrible weapon. As long as you build, you will live. Stop and you will die."

Sarah Pardee Winchester arrived in San Jose, California, in 1884, where she purchased an eight-room farmhouse that stood on one hundred and sixty-two acres of land. She immediately hired twenty-two carpenters who commenced adding ten rooms to the house.

As the structure mushroomed to twenty-six rooms, railroad cars were switched onto a nearby siding where their cargos of rich imported furnishings were unloaded and wagoned to the Winchester mansion.

The Widow Winchester had no master plan for the construction work. She built however and whatever she so chose. In addition to her score or more of carpenters, she hired a staff of twelve to eighteen gardeners and field hands. As the sounds of hammers and saws echoed around the clock, the house grew and grew.

Each morning she met with her foreman, and they went over the plans for that day's work. Sometimes, when things didn't work out as anticipated, Sarah would just build another room around an existing one. But where did she get her ideas?

One of the first rooms added to the original eight-room farmhouse was a séance room. It was located on the second floor in the middle of the house. There were no outside windows in the séance room. Sarah held séances without the benefit of mediums. She had the only key to the blue-colored meditation room. No one else was allowed to enter the chamber. Thirteen different ceremonial robes hung from thirteen different hooks in the blue room. Her procedure was to retire to her séance room and sit there until the spirits put structural ideas into her head. Sarah would ponder the ideas, write them down on paper and then have her secretary put them into effect.

A bell tower holding a large church-type bell was erected. It was unscalable, and the bell toller's rope hung down through the inside of the tower shaft to a secret room in the cellar accessible through an underground labyrinth known only to a Japanese servant and his apprentice. The bell ringer carried an expensive pocket watch, and in his quarters were three of the best chronometers available. Each day he telephoned an astronomical observatory in order to check the accuracy of his watch and chronometers.

Some people, today, say that the purpose of the bell was to summon the field hands to work. If that was so, why was Sarah Winchester so concerned about the split-second accuracy of the bell toller's timepiece? Actually, according to some records, the bell would toll at the stroke of midnight, at one o'clock in the morning and again at two o'clock in the morning, then remain silent the rest of the twenty-four hours! Did Sarah Winchester have the bells tolled at those hours to summon the spirits to her séances? From her studies of ghost lore, or possibly from the spirits themselves, the widow became aware that the element of time was of deep importance concerning the arrival, expected or otherwise, of visitors from another dimension.

Day after day, week after week, and year after year, the size of the house grew. There were stairways that led only to blank ceilings, hallways which led to noplace. Cabinets opened onto solid walls.

Why Sarah had forty-seven fireplaces installed is not known. Possibly it had something to do with her spiritualistic thinking. There is much evidence of the widow's belief in spiritualism. The number "13" is almost universally accepted as an evil and unlucky number. But in centuries past it was considered unlucky only for evil persons. Thus, Mrs. Winchester's workers were concerned that everywhere in the growing house she was intrigued by the number "13." Nearly all of the windows held thirteen panes of glass; thirteen palm trees lined the drive; the greenhouse had thirteen cupolas; the walls had thirteen panels; the wooden floor of the ballroom was sectioned in blocks of thirteen squares; there would be thirteen bathrooms; many of the ceilings had thirteen panels; there were rooms with thirteen windows; most of the stairway banisters were supported by thirteen inverted stanchions; and every staircase but one had thirteen steps. The exception is a winding staircase with forty-two steps, enough to take the climber up at least three stories. But these forty-two steps reached an elevation of only nine feet, for each step was but two inches high.

Room by room the mansion expanded to castle-like proportions. Her fear of the curse of death kept the hammers and saws going around the clock day in and day out including Christmas. Workers stayed on the job for years because of the unusually high salaries they received.

There were times when Sarah may have felt that death was near, for she would suddenly add a dozen new workers to those already there.

Very few guests visited the ever-expanding house. That is, very few earthly guests. For who else would be welcomed to a house with doors that led to nowhere, windows that opened to blankness, stairs that ascended to nothing, and a bell that tolled, supposedly, only during the witching hour?

Indian-slayers of the Old West used to brag that the only good Indian was a dead Indian. But for Sarah Winchester, a dead one was the worst kind. The maze of confusion that dominated the architecture of the Winchester house was obviously designed to confuse and discourage the vengeful spirits of the redmen who perished at the wrong end of "the gun that won the West."

Each night just before the stroke of twelve, as Mrs. Winchester set out for her séance room, she would trek the meandering hallways on a route that would defy the ghost of the most experienced Indian tracker. After traversing an interminable intricacy of rooms and passageways, the widow would suddenly push a concealed button. A panel would open, and she would pass through the secret opening into another room. Unless a pursuing spirit was quick and alert, he would lose her. Next she would open a window and step through it—not to the outside but into another room and thence down a flight of stairs that took her down to the next floor only to meet another set of steps that led right back up to the same level again. And back up she would go, convinced that the ghosts of the simple redmen had become discouraged.

She would lock herself in the séance room, don the appropriate ceremonial robe and wait for the stroke of midnight.

There are no windows in the séance room, only light shafts leading in at various angles. A closet door on one wall opens to a closet that isn't. The table was bare except for paper and pencil (probably for automatic writing) and a planchette board.

It's not known what took place in the séance room at the stroke of midnight, or whether or not the spirits called by Sarah ever came. But if they did, they discussed the construction of the house and its design. Mrs. Winchester wrote it all down.

At the ringing of two o'clock in the morning on the bell, the spirits returned to wherever spirits go when they are not haunting. And with the coming of morning, the widow and her construction foreman would go over the plans developed during the night's séance.

Hammers pounded and saws hacked away. New floors were added, rooms were built inside other rooms and, by 1906, the house was a towering seven stories tall.

On sleepless nights when she wasn't holding critiques with the spirit world, Sarah Winchester would play her grand piano into the wee hours of the morning. Passersby would admire the strains of music permeating the night air, even though two piano keys were out of tune.

During the daylight hours, when she wasn't inspecting the construction work, Sarah would spend long intervals in the "Daisy Room" (so-called because of the daisies in the stained-glass windows in that room). From that second-floor room she would watch the wagons and horseless carriages pass by. She liked the Daisy Room so much that it became not only her favorite daytime room but also her preferred bedroom. That is—until April 18, 1906. On that night, as Sarah lay awake pondering the pace of the construction going on about the house, her bed began to shake. In the dim glow of the gaslight she watched in horror as plaster on the walls cracked before her very eyes. Then the whole house began to crumble. She was certain that the spirits of the thousands of Indians who fell before Winchester rifles had finally come for her soul. As ceiling beams came crashing down, she screamed in terror. Sarah struggled toward the door, but her way was blocked by a fallen timber. She clawed, she panicked and she fainted.

The great 1906 San Francisco earthquake had struck. When the tremors subsided, the Winchester house was in shambles. The top three floors of the seven-story structure had collapsed into the garden.

It was hours before Sarah's servants were able to free her from the Daisy Room. She immediately ordered that room boarded up and sealed off from the rest of the house. And it so remained for the next sixteen years. Neither she nor anyone else set foot in it. It became a "forgotten" room.

With the earthquake damage repaired, expansion of the house continued. The number of bedrooms increased from fifteen to twenty, and from twenty to twenty-five. There were chimneys all over the place—many serving no purpose whatsoever except that spooks prefer to enter or vanish via chimneys, if ghost stories are to be believed. Only two mirrors were installed in the entire house, probably because Sarah believed that spirits had a fear of their own reflections and would immediately vanish upon seeing them. The secretary and servants apparently either used hand mirrors or went without.

Dozens of skylights were installed throughout the house. Some opened to the outside world while others merely opened from one room to the next—having been installed in the middle of a floor.

On and on went the endless construction of the Winchester house. No blueprints were ever used. The work was done from sketches made by Sarah and her spiritual friends on wrapping paper and even table-cloths.

But not everything in the Winchester house reflected eccentricity. Sarah was ingenious in many ways. Some of her ideas and innovations were decades ahead of their time. In nearly every room she had an annunciator installed to enable her to signal her whereabouts to the servants—or vice versa. The power for gas and electricity was generated in a plant directly on the grounds. She invented a crank that would open and close shutters from inside. Winchester House was one of the first structures to utilize wool insulation. The row of washtubs in the huge laundry had built-in scrub boards. Sarah developed a tamper-proof window latch patterned after the trigger mechanism of the Winchester rifle. Every door required a different key to open; the keys in their totality filled three large buckets. But were all the locks and latches necessary?

Nearly every burglar on the Pacific slope knew of the "treasure-laden" safes in Sarah Winchester's home. Yet none ever attempted to rob the mansion. For a thief would be loath to enter a house unless he knew the exact locations of the valuables and every door and window. Had a burglar entered the Winchester house, he would have gone stark, raving mad trying to find his way about that ghostly house in the dark.

While dining in secluded splendor with her secretary, Sarah enjoyed sipping on rare imported wines and liqueurs. In one of the two basements was a wine cellar that would have put most spirit shops (the drinking kind) to shame.

One afternoon, Sarah went down to the wine cellar to inventory her stock. Moments later, she came flying back upstairs, screaming all the way. On the cellar wall there was a black imprint of a hand; she was sure this came as a warning from a spirit-world demon as a symbol of the evils of alcohol. To no avail, servants told her that it was merely the handprint of a workman which had been there for many years. Without removing the contents, she had the entrance to the wine cellar bricked up, and so hidden by subsequent structures that to this day the treasure of wine and liqueur has never been found.

As the years went by the Winchester house continued to expand. Many of the original workers and artisans retired or died. But sons and grandsons carried on. Some rooms were so completely hidden by other rooms that the former were virtually lost forever.

On September 4, 1922, after a session with her spirit friends in the séance room, Sarah Pardee Winchester retired for the night. Sometime during the early morning hours of September 5, the tiny woman died in her sleep at the age of eighty-three.

Rumors told of Sarah's having a thirty-thousand-dollar solid gold dinner service and a quantity of jewelry in her safes. When relatives forced open the safes (only Sarah had known the combinations), they found old fishlines, some socks, newspaper clippings from years before telling of the deaths of her daughter and husband, a box filled with a lock of baby hair and a suit of woolen underwear. No solid gold dinner service was found.

Relatives removed the furniture and Sarah's personal belongings before selling the house to a group of investors who planned to use it as a tourist attraction. Among those who visited the Winchester house when it was first opened to the public were Harry Houdini and Robert Ripley.

It was first advertised as a one-hundred-and-forty-eight-room mystery house. But so confusing were the layout and floor plan that every time a room count was taken, a different total was arrived at. It took five years and dozens of recounts before it was decided that there were one hundred and sixty rooms in the Winchester house. Today, no one is still exactly sure that the figure of one hundred and sixty is correct. The house has been declared a California Historical Landmark and is registered with the National Park Service as a large, odd dwelling with an unknown number of rooms.

As we pulled up in the driveway around closing time, Nancy and I were greeted by Keith Kittle, administrator of the Winchester Mystery House.

"So, you're the writers who want to risk a night in the Winchester Mystery House," he said.

After the introductions and other formalities, we were shown through the chaotic maze of rooms. The mood of the rooms varied from sunny and cheerful to drab and dismal. Our young female guide told us the story of the house's history as she escorted us about.

We were led into the séance room. When Nancy told our escort that we were to spend the night in there, she replied, "Oh, this room is not too scary. I wouldn't be afraid to spend the night in here—at least if someone else was with me."

"I thought this place was supposed to be so spooky?" I said.

"It's the Daisy Room in front that frightens me," the guide answered. "I wouldn't spend a night in there for anything. That's the room where Sarah Winchester was trapped during the 1906 earthquake."

"What's so frightening about it?" asked Nancy.

"I can't really pinpoint any one thing," replied the guide. "But sometimes that room gets so chilly. Not the whole room but just in certain parts. And there's that feeling when I'm in there alone like maybe I'm being watched, like I'm not alone. Some of the others who work here have told me that they get the same feeling in that room. Sometimes it's . . ."

"That's the room we're going to stay in tonight!" I interrupted.

No tourists or guides crowded noisily around the

grounds as we pulled back into the empty parking lot at the Winchester Mystery House later that night. But two enormous German shepherd attack dogs came charging toward where we stood. Snarling and barking, fangs bared, they lunged at us, only to be repelled by a high-chain link fence that protected the grounds from intruders—and intruders from the dogs.

As we neared the main entrance, I glanced skyward at the full witch's moon that looked more like a round glowing hole in the velvet black sky. Only the snarling of the dogs disturbed the silence of the night.

While we stood waiting near the main entrance, a shadowy figure emerged from the inner recesses of the huge mystery house. We felt reassured when the shape proved to be the man we were supposed to meet. He unbolted the door and beckoned us in, locking the door behind us.

We exchanged greetings and he led us along the dimly lit entrance hall. As we followed him through a maze of darkened rooms illuminated only by his flashlight, Nancy moved alongside the security guard and asked, "Before you take us upstairs, could we ask you a few questions about your personal experiences here?"

The young man, who gave the impression that he was recently out of the military service, pushed a shock of black hair out of his eyes, hesitated for a moment and replied, "Sure, but I'd prefer that my name not be used. My wife and I both live on the grounds and we'd rather not be bothered by publicity."

Raising the tape recorder Nancy asked, "Have you yourself ever experienced anything strange or unusual in here?"

He stopped at the foot of the stairs, turned to face Nancy and said, "Last month we had a rash of false alarms every night for a week. We just couldn't come up with an answer to what was triggering the alarm system. Now, my father-in-law is a full-blooded Indian and he told me it was the spirits. I don't believe in ghosts but I respect his beliefs, so when he said to ask the spirits to stop, I did. Sure enough, we haven't had a single false alarm since!

"My wife won't come in this place, though. She's half-Indian and pretty psychic. She sees and hears things, but I just don't want to fool around with stuff like that.

"At night, I can hear footsteps and sounds when no one's here. But this is an old house and it doesn't pay for me to worry about things I can't see. So, I try to ignore them."

It was clear that our line of questioning was making our host nervous. He brushed off our attempts to question him further about the noises he had heard and began to elaborate on the security system as he beckoned us to follow him up the darkened stairway.

A distinct chill greeted us as we entered the Daisy Room. It was already after eleven as we put our equipment down and spread our mats on the room's hardwood floor.

As the security director reached the door, he turned and said, "Don't forget now! Don't go downstairs, because if that alarm goes off, you'll have every cop in San Jose converging on this house. If something happens and you need help, just pick up the phone at the top of the stairs just outside the room. It rings down in my cottage . . . I'll hear it—if I'm not sleeping too soundly." He left.

A second later he stuck his head back through the door. "By the way," he said. "Don't stand up in front of the street-side windows—especially with your flashlight on."

"Why?" I asked.

"Well," he replied, "see those holes in the glass? They're bullet holes. And you can see right up here on the wall where the bullets lodged. Sniper fire," he went on.

Nancy and I exchanged glances and quickly

dropped to our mats. We kept a low profile as we prepared for a long night. I stretched out on my mat (there was no furniture in the room), but either the floor was too hard or the mat was too thin; I got back up and began wandering around the room. As I was thinking how much better I'd feel if there were electric lights on the second floor, I felt a sudden chill. When I moved away from the cold spot, the room was warm again. But when I backed up, the chill was still at the same spot.

"Hey, Nancy," I said, "come here and stand in this area. It's about ten degrees colder than the rest of the room. There's gotta be a draft coming in right here from someplace!"

She rose to her feet, walked over to where I stood and held her hand over the cold spot. "Look around," she said, "do you see any place where a draft could possibly be coming in?"

She was right. There was no opening or anything else that could be creating a draft. In fact, the cold air wasn't moving. It was just a still mass of cold atmosphere covering about the area that a human body would occupy were it standing there.

Holding both arms extended out in front of her body, palms down, Nancy looked straight ahead and said, "It's a presence."

"A presence?" I asked. "Who's present?"

Without turning her head toward me, she replied, "There's a concentration of psychic energy here. We're not alone."

"Well, seeing is believing," I commented. "It's just like that news item we heard on the radio this afternoon about the seer who predicted that San Francisco's going to have a moderate to severe earthquake tomorrow. When I see it, I'll believe it. But as far as I'm concerned now, that reporter is just another sensationalist making a guess, like those so-called psychics whose predictions are always spread over the front page of those national scandal papers. And with that, my dear, I think I'm going to bug out. It's been a long day."

Not turning from the cold spot, Nancy said, "Say what you want about the person who predicted the earthquake. But while you're lying there trying to fall asleep, think about this having been the room in which Sarah Winchester was trapped during the 1906 earthquake. Keep the camera and tape recorder ready." I dozed off.

"Wake up! Wake up! Listen, do you hear it?"

Although it was almost two in the morning, I felt as though I'd been dozing only for minutes when I felt Nancy shaking me.

"Hear what?" I asked.

"The music, the music!" she answered. "Someone's playing the piano. Can't you hear it? It's coming from somewhere down that hall."

Just as I was about to tell her that I couldn't hear anything, the floor began shaking. "Feel the floor, it's shaking!" I exclaimed.

"The whole place is trembling," replied Nancy as she shone her flashlight about the room.

The tremor lasted but half a minute. Then everything was still again. "Well," I commented, "I guess I owe that psychic an apology. He didn't do bad on his earthquake prediction. He got the right day, but he was just a few hours off. I wonder how much damage happened up in Frisco."

"That piano music was so beautiful," said Nancy. "It sounded as though it was being played by a concert pianist—except for two flat keys."

"Sarah Winchester's piano was supposed to have had two flat keys," I replied.

I'm not certain whether or not it was the coldness of the night or what had just happened that kept us awake until nearly dawn.

About four in the morning, Nancy again heard the piano music. I couldn't hear it, however. But a few minutes later we both heard footsteps in the hall just

outside the Daisy Room. The beam of our flashlights picked up nothing. As Nancy struggled with
one of the tape recorders, I took two quick-flash
pictures down the hallway.

I don't remember how much later it was, but as
I looked out the window I could see the first streaks
of dawn to the east.

As the gray light began to fill the outside-facing
rooms, I got up, took one of the tape recorders and a
camera, and told Nancy that I was going to explore
parts of the second and third floors. She didn't
answer, for she was cuddled between the two mats
fast asleep.

I neither saw nor heard anything as I moved down
the hallway. Exploring one room after another, I
eventually came across the séance room. It seemed
very warm—much warmer than the rest of the house
and almost to the point of being hot. When I walked
back out of that blue-painted room, I could again
feel the chill night air.

But even more astounding than that was the fact
that when I crossed a room, I couldn't hear my footsteps. Through some strange phenomenon, the floors
would creak a second or two *after* I walked across
them. It made me wonder whether it was really
just the delayed action of creaking floor timbers, the
result of some quirk in the construction, or footsteps
of a spirit following me.

I went back for Nancy and brought her out to
where the delayed-footstep phenomenon occurred.
But when I tried to show her what happened, we
could hear only my footsteps and the floor creaking
under my shoes as I took each step. There was no
delayed-action effect.

"Good morning, there. How'd it go?" It was one
of the janitors.

After explaining to him about the footstep incident
and listening to his own stories of similar occurrences,
I asked, "How much damage did the earthquake
do?"

"What earthquake?" he asked.

"The earthquake about two o'clock this morning," I responded. "It felt like the whole house was shaking."

"Must have slept through it," he answered as he went about his work.

When we checked, we found that there was no earthquake anyplace in California during the hours that Nancy and I were in the Winchester house. Seismographs throughout the state recorded absolutely nothing.

Is it possible that the mass of psychic energy we felt in the Daisy Room might have been the spirit return of Sarah Winchester? Could it be that from time to time her spirit relives the great 1906 earthquake that trapped her in that room? If so, was the night that Nancy and I chose to spend in the Winchester Mystery House one of the times that the terrible earthquake of 1906 reoccurred—*in the spirit world?*

Don't cry ... Which do you think
it'll hurt the most? Oh God!
You think I want to be a ghost? ...

John V.A. Weaver

4

The Whaley House—
The House on
the Hanging Ground

The Whaley House is located at 2482 San Diego
Avenue. It is a hundred-and-twenty-year-old structure which was occupied by Whaleys or their
descendants from 1856, when it was built by Thomas
Whaley, to 1953. In appearance, it is not an impres-
sive home but looks very friendly and comfortable.
There is an absence of that oppressive feeling of
malevolence so noticeable in most haunted houses.
Its construction is representative of many western
houses built during the mid-1800's, and therein lies
the charm of the Whaley House. The house is nestled
in the heart of San Diego's preservation-restoration
area reminiscent of the wild and wooly Old West.

Mrs. June A. Reading, director of the Whaley
House, is a bright and attractive woman, and a most
cooperative and knowledgeable lady. She greeted us
cordially and spent hours reviewing various episodes
of a psychic nature that had transpired at the
Whaley House, then asked if we had any specific
questions.

"Ghostly manifestations are usually associated with

human tragedy," said Richard. "It doesn't seem to me that Thomas Whaley had more problems than other citizens of his time. How did his house get haunted?"

"Well, part of the Whaley House was the county courtroom from 1869 until 1871. Thomas Whaley had part of this house modified to be a courtroom. Then, after only several years of use, a decision was made by the city fathers to move the court records to New Town, a more developed part of San Diego which is now the downtown area. Well, Mr. Whaley put up a terrific fight to stop the transfer of records but town officials came in the dead of night and took everything. Thomas Whaley didn't think that was fair. He wasn't even reimbursed for all the work he'd done on the courtroom. He died before the matter was settled. That's a pretty good excuse for a restless spirit, don't you think?

"And, you must remember, the Whaleys lived through lynchings, Indian uprisings and other exciting happenings; so there was sufficient emotional attachment to this house to cause it to be haunted. With five generations of Whaleys having lived and died here, this place is like a huge reservoir of family memories. There's a very concentrated force present just from the Whaleys, and the history of the land itself before the construction of the home is pretty gory, too!"

"What about 'Yankee Jim,' the man who was hanged on this site? He'd make a much more interesting ghost, don't you think? Maybe he's the man the people get shadowy glimpses of on the landing," offered Richard, somewhat hopefully.

"Yankee Jim would have good reason to return as an angry spirit," insisted June. "They hanged him right over there," she said, pointing to the arch between the parlor and music room as the site of the old gallows. "This house was built on the very site where he was hanged. In all honesty, he wasn't hanged, he was strangled to death. You really couldn't call it a hanging—it took him at least forty minutes to die, swinging and kicking the air and gasping for breath. Poor soul!

"It was a crudely constructed gallows and Yankee Jim was a taller man than most. Because he had charisma, he thought he'd just talk his way out of the hanging. But they whipped the horses right out from under him, right in the middle of his farewell speech. They hanged him from a wagon bed, since they didn't have a proper gallows platform."

"Whatever did he do to deserve such a terrible punishment?" I asked.

"The law was harsh in 1852, and frontier justice dealt swiftly with offenders," June continued. "The town was experiencing a crime wave. William Marshall and Juan Verdugo were hanged for murder and treason for their complicity in an Indian uprising, and six months later James 'Yankee Jim' Robinson was found guilty of trying to steal a schooner called the *Plutas* from the San Diego harbor. At that time, there was a law to the effect that if anyone stole over two hundred dollars he could be sentenced to death. And they decided to make an example of Yankee Jim. Stealing a boat in this seafaring town was just as bad as stealing a horse in the days of the Old West.

"Strangling to death is a bad way to go. But when he was finally dead, they cut him down and took his body out and planted it in an unmarked grave— just shoveled the dirt over him. He didn't even get a respectable Christian burial. Some people think the mysterious footsteps heard in the house belong to Yankee Jim. Corinne Lillian Whaley, Thomas Whaley's daughter, died here in 1953 at a ripe old age. She refused to go upstairs because there was something up on that floor she didn't like. She never did explain what it was that scared her."

"Maybe it was the ghost of Yankee Jim," said Richard. "And if it was, then he surely must have made his presence known to the Whaleys. So we can't really say that nothing traumatic happened to the family. It might well be that Yankee Jim himself is responsible for the other ghosts or apparitions that hang around the house."

"We know about the past ghostly happenings at Whaley House. What about current goings-on? Has anything new happened?" I asked.

"Well," said June, "the guides have reported the smell of lighted cigars—not ordinary cigars but expensive Havanas. This is a wooden structure and no one is allowed to smoke in here. We have heat-sensing devices set up throughout the place, but the tobacco smoke doesn't trigger the alarm. When the cigar smoke is detected and everyone runs around looking for the guy with the lighted cigar, he is never found!

"Then, too, there's the sound of horses hoofs. The horses come right up to the gate and stop, but nothing's ever there. You get accustomed to things like that around here. Sometimes we smell perfume, a very strong perfume. The fragrance was verified by a reporter who came to do a story. You never know when these things will happen at Whaley House.

"There's a rocking chair that rocks all by itself, and many visitors have heard the sound of a child crying. One visitor who was a mother said it sounded like the cry of a sick baby, and the crying does always come from the nursery. In five generations of Whaleys, there were probably plenty of sick babies in that room.

"And on May 6, 1977, one of our volunteer guides, Ms. Dorothy Tyson, entered the house early one morning and heard the sound of music coming from the music room. Naturally it startled her. She checked the streets to see if there was music coming from a passing car. But that early in the morning the streets were deserted."

Most everyone in San Diego has heard rumors about the Whaley House being haunted. One day, the San Diego Historical Society lent June Reading two workmen to help set up exhibits on the second floor. It was early morning and the three of them were waiting downstairs for a furniture delivery. Eyes converged upward when they heard the sounds of a man's heavy footsteps from the upper floor. The two workmen became very disturbed and obviously frightened. June reassured them that other county employees had duplicate keys and were probably upstairs cleaning up in preparation for the furniture delivery. To put her helpers at ease, she walked to the top of the stairs and discovered no visible presence on the second level. Then she went back downstairs to rejoin her companions. "There's no one up there," she said.

The two wide-eyed workmen exchanged knowing glances. One man said half in jest and half sincerely, "Probably old Thomas Whaley's come back to look this place over." The solemnity of the moment was forgotten and everyone had a good laugh.

"Is the psychic activity here constant or periodical? Is it more pronounced during one season than others?" said Richard.

"In fall and winter months, when the house is relatively quiet, there is more ghostly activity," said June. "From the time school begins until about January, there are plenty of things happening here. Of course, the Whaleys, being a big family, put great stock in Thanksgiving and Christmas celebrations. It was their custom to enjoy the holidays together.

"It's interesting that sounds are manifest here more often than images. Regis Philbin, a gentleman from a local television station, once saw the apparition of a woman. A lady's face materialized out of an energy mass which he thought was the likeness of Anna Whaley, Thomas Whaley's wife.

"There's an area in the study that seems to be an energy source or battery for producing psychical phenomena. There are cold spots in the study and in the kitchen toward the back of the house. At times the cold spots are so apparent that visitors become alarmed and will comment on them."

She gestured toward the door and went on: "Since a recent burglary, nothing can be opened from the outside at Whaley House without keys. Windows are nailed shut, new bolts are on the doors and everything is kept under lock and key on the main floor. So there's no possibility of air circulating unless the front door is open and there is a strong breeze coming through, which is not usually the case. Normally, the front door is kept closed.

"The night Regis saw the apparition, he was seated in the parlor, and I remember him saying the energy form developed in the study. One cold spot was on one side of the desk and another luminous energy mass was on the wall. It didn't do anything but move back and forth—expanding and contracting. When the light was right, it could easily be seen and it always hovered around Mr. Whaley's desk. We watched the mass for a long period and it never moved away from the desk, nor did it form into a figure.

"We also saw a similar undulating energy mass in the courtroom. My husband and I sat on a Whaley settee in the courtroom with the room darkened at Regis' request. Most of the furniture in the Whaley House is donated and belonged to the Whaley family. We both watched the thing from the settee as it moved back and forth, expanding and contracting. The energy form had a luminous quality—even in the dark room it was visible!

"The energy mass moved through the music room and started toward the parlor. It was then that the parapsychologists and witnesses who were present saw a human face centered in the most concentrated area of the psychic energy mass. Everyone was so amazed and even a little frightened. Someone flashed a flashlight on it and that spoiled it."

Glancing toward a window, Mrs. Reading continued: "It was in August, two years ago, that we had a very humid condition with a great deal of static electricity present. We began to notice the most interesting energy forms developing in the Whaley girls' bedroom upstairs. We really can't say what caused it to form in that particular room. These forms were so sharp that we were able to get pictures of them with a thirty-five-millimeter camera. The little shafts of light looked like fireflies darting around the room.

"Parapsychologists consider these luminous flashes of light to be ectoplasmic tubes of energy. They think that if enough of these extensions are visible, a manifestation, or materialization, from the other world can happen."

"Could you make out anything from the energy forms?" asked Richard.

"Yes," she exclaimed. "We could finally see, out of focus, the upper part of a woman's body! The outline was sharp enough so that you could see some movement in the arms. She was either folding clothes or packing things at the end of the bed. It was a woman, but the rest of the figure didn't develop. It was a partial figure."

"Did you get a photograph?" asked Richard.

June shook her head apologetically. "No, we didn't, but we certainly tried! I gave it some thought and decided that the only thing that allowed us to even see the ghost in the first place was a wardrobe that provided a perfect background."

Richard, the perennial skeptic, asked, "Did anyone else see the activity?"

"Yes," she said, "that's the exciting part. Tourists who were visiting the house that day all saw the ectoplasmic tubes darting around the room."

"Surely, with so much happening, you got at least one clear picture. After all, seeing is believing, right?"

Without a moment's hesitation, and with considerable enthusiasm, June Reading rejoined, "Yes, you're right! And we did take some slides of the ectoplasmic tubes of light. When the slides were enlarged we could easily make out an aura around them. So, we do have that much physical evidence. And, of course, there are the sounds."

"The sounds?" Richard asked.

"Yes, the sounds," she replied. "Sounds are never dissipated, you know. There were five generations of Whaleys who lived and died in this home, and I believe anything of emotional importance can be heard again and again under the right conditions. For instance, the deep, hearty laughter of a man is sometimes heard upstairs. I've heard it myself. Another guide who was with me heard it, too."

"What were the weather conditions when you heard the laughter?" questioned Richard.

"Well, there was a very heavy rain that day. The house was extremely quiet. The rain continued all through the day and business was at a complete standstill. It was during Christmas vacation and the guides were downstairs chatting. All of them heard the walking sounds, not once but twice that day. When I went upstairs to investigate, one of the girls went with me—just as a precaution.

"There was only one light, and that was in the Whaley children's nursery. But everything was untouched—except that the master bedroom window was wide open. But the shutters were closed. It's a tall, heavy wooden window, and was saturated and swollen with the day's humidity and almost too much for me to handle. Satisfied that no vandal had been up there, we went to the nursery and I showed my companion a little porcelain doll that was tucked away in a dresser drawer. Suddenly, it got very dark and I thought the storm must be getting worse. Then I heard the unmistakable baritone laughter of a man —very pleasant laughter, nothing sinister, but it was there. The girl who was with me turned and said, 'Did you hear that?'

"One of our guides," continued June, "described a figure of a man standing on the landing, and the description fits Thomas Whaley—size, period clothing, everything exactly fits Thomas Whaley."

> Now, am I Chuang Tzu who has dreamed
> that he was a butterfly,
> Or am I a butterfly which is now
> dreaming that he is Chuang Tzu?
> Chuang Tzu
> Ancient Chinese Philosopher

5

Erotic Entities

Many occultists, religious sects and spiritualists believe that sexual dreams to the point of climax are in reality spiritual seduction or, in simpler words, sex with a ghost.

From medieval days up to colonial times, wet dreams were considered to be a seduction by Satan, and the dreamer could be tried for witchcraft.

In the July 1978 issue of *Forum* magazine,* there appeared a letter titled "Out of This World." With the permission of Forum International, Ltd., we are reproducing the letter in part:

"I am 33, single, in reasonable good health and of sound mind. I mention my sanity because the story I want to relate will sound incredible to most people—the product of an extremely fertile imagination—yet my experience, while truly unique, did in fact happen. You see, I was made love to by a ghost!

"It happened last fall, while I was vacationing in England. I spent the first few days of my vacation

---

*Reprinted from *Forum*, July 1978. Copyright © 1978 by Forum International, Ltd. Reprinted by permission.

sightseeing in London, and then, because I wanted to explore the lovely English countryside, I took a room in a charming old inn in Devon. With its warm turn-of-the-century ambiance, a sturdy-looking bar of burnished wood, and a crackling fire in the fireplace, I thought it was the perfect setting for someone who wanted to soak up the atmosphere of Merrie Olde England. The guests were friendly and certainly didn't mind having an American in their midst.

"My first night at the inn was uneventful—I had spent the day on a walking tour of the countryside. I spent the second day as I had the first, roaming about the mist-covered countryside, and returned to the inn that evening totally exhausted. By 11 p.m. I was sound asleep.

"In the middle of the night (I have no idea of the exact time) I was coaxed out of sleep by what sounded like the rustling of leaves. Something told me I was not alone in the room. I could hear my heart start to pound as I looked toward the open window. The curtains billowed in the breeze. My eyes scanned the room. It was dark, the silence eerie. Then I heard the rustling again. It was coming closer, moving slowly, irrevocably, to the bed.

"And then I went all goosebumps when I saw a pale, shadowy apparition, a faint, all but imperceptible semblance of a female form.

"I shook my head vigorously side to side, convinced that by so doing I would rouse myself from this dream. But no, I wasn't dreaming. This was real. I was wide awake, fists clenched at my sides, wondering what would happen next. Curiously enough, I didn't panic. It never occurred to me to be afraid. Perhaps I was simply mesmerized by the other-worldliness of it all.

"Suddenly, a pair of soft, succulent lips were pressing against mine. But there was no face, no body! I brought my hands up off the bed and felt for flesh. Nothing. A tongue slithered into my mouth and entwined itself with mine.

"The tongue finally withdrew from my mouth and those lovely lips left mine. A moment later that tongue was worming its way down my chest, to my stomach, ——."

The writer then went on to describe a most erotic sexual experience that could well teach Linda Lovelace a thing or two!

"I had to pinch myself to prove I wasn't dreaming. My eyes strained in the darkness to discern a recognizable feature, a face, hair, anything. I reached toward the apparition. I moved my hands back and forth where her body had to be. Nothing but air.

"I gave up trying to figure it out and surrendered to the pleasure."

The man's letter becomes most descriptive and is typical of experiences reported by others. He goes on:

"She moved slowly at first, with a steady, unhurried rhythm, as if she knew what she was doing. Then, gradually, the tempo increased, until I had the climax of my life. I don't mean it as a pun, but it was truly out of this world. Let me tell you, that lady ghost, whatever or whoever she was, knew her business. She was highly knowledgeable in the art of love.

"After my unbelievable orgasm, I waited expectantly, hoping that now that it was over, she would speak, explain, show herself to me. But nothing. The shadowy female form left the bed, the soft sound of rustling leaves accompanying her as she floated off toward one wall. And then, as I stared in utter disbelief, she disappeared into the wall!

"I reached down and felt the sheet, fully expecting to find evidence of our eerie coupling. Imagine my surprise when I found that it was dry, not a trace of semen! What happened to my ejaculate—where had it gone? There was only one explanation. My ghost girl had obviously taken it with her.

"Needless to say, I didn't sleep a wink the rest of the night. When morning came, I hurried downstairs. I was bursting to tell somebody, anybody, about what had happened to me. I found one of the men I had met my first day at the inn sitting at a table having coffee. I rushed over to him, sat down, and blurted out my story. When I was finished, he laughed. Just as I thought. He didn't believe a word of it.

"'But I do believe you,' he said with a broad smile. 'That sexy little bitch must have been in the mood for a handsome American. I only wish it had been me with her last night.'

"Thoroughly confused, I asked for an explanation. 'Didn't you know?' he said. 'This inn is haunted. That's right, haunted. Seems that around the turn of the century a married barmaid worked here. A real oversexed wench she was. Anyway, one night her husband caught her poking another chap and in a fit of rage, killed her. Murdered her on the spot. But her spirit lives on, you see, and from time to time she selects a guest and gives him the time of his life. Men come from miles around just to spend a night here, all in hope of making it with her.' My friend chuckled. 'Most of them, though, don't stand a ghost of a chance with her.'

"Well, that's my story, as unbelievable as it sounds. Before I went to England, I didn't believe in ghosts. But after my experience there, I'm all for ghosts, especially the female variety.

R. P.
California"

The late Dr. Nathan Fodor, psychoanalyst, educator, psychic investigator and author, told of an amazing series of incidents involving a Long Island woman back in the early 1960's. The lady, whom he referred to as Jean, contacted the psychoanalyst after seeing him on a New York City television talk show. She told how she was being seduced by a nightly visitor. The phantom lover had even made advances on the twenty-six-year-old woman's middle-aged mother.

The psychoanalyst met with Jean and her mother and learned that the amorous apparition was someone whom Jean had known when he was alive. She was a writer, and he was a medical doctor. They had known each other only casually and they had never dated. It was shortly after his thirty-fourth birthday that John died after a brief illness. "On the day John died," said the young woman, "I felt his presence and heard his voice call, 'I'm not dead.'"

She sat down on her bed a day later and felt someone sitting next to her. She even saw an impression forming in the mattress, although there was no person there. He began caressing her. As time passed, the entity became more intimate. It was only a matter of time before they were making love. "It was," she said, "the most rapturous delight I've ever experienced."

Eventually, the ecstasy implicit in the situation began reaching a point where John was controlling her complete life. There were, however, some practical features. John, having been a doctor, suggested that Jean take Pirodixin for her chronic acne. It helped. If she was stuck for a word while writing, John would suddenly come out with the right word. He was actually dictating her life-style. He began to resent her dating.

She began to notice a disagreeable odor in his presence. She referred to it as "a male sex odor." She began to feel his hands all over her body—even in public places. Sometimes he'd cause her to have an orgasm while she was talking to people who were totally unaware of her ghostly lover. Needless to say, she found it most embarrassing. She even began experiencing his presence while riding the subway.

Jean's mother began sleeping with her daughter, hoping that her presence in the bed would keep John away. But John began making passes at the mother.

An exorcism was performed in the house. That very night John returned. "He was jumping up and down on the bed to show that he was not exorcised," said Jean.

She took a large metal crucifix and bent it in such a way that she could wear it as a chastity belt. That stopped him for a day. "I took it off and got into the bathtub. While I was getting out, he was rubbing against me. To stop him, I put the crucifix back on in a hurry.

"The beast has been attacking my rear continuously," she told the psychoanalyst. "It makes me sick." A séance was held in the hope of talking to John and getting him to leave. But he wouldn't talk or materialize. However, his presence began to weaken. His visits became less frequent.

Then one night, after John had been gone for some weeks, Jean was riding in a car with some friends. The driver fell asleep at the wheel. Jean was half asleep and was unaware of the driver's situation. Suddenly she felt John's presence. An instant later, the driver woke up crying, "Someone pinched me. Who was it? If I hadn't been awakened at that instant, we would have run off the road and crashed."

John had returned. The last the psychoanalyst heard, Jean and John were back together. Whether or not they're still together now after fifteen years is not known.

Another woman who prefers ghostly lovers to human beaus is twenty-year-old Jenny P. of Birmingham, England. "He's been seeing me for over three years," said Jenny of her lover. "We make love three times a week. I'm not interested in human boyfriends. They don't compare with my ghost."

There are probably many varying reasons why an individual would indulge in sex with a spiritual entity. A letter received from Ms. L.L. of Florida gives a clue as to what kind of circumstances would motivate a ghostly love affair:

"In my early adulthood, my religious belief was

fundamentalistic. I adhered strictly to the letter of biblical law, even though doing so made me unpopular with my husband, my family and friends.

"When I was twenty-two, I became a Jehovah's Witness, a very fundamental sect of Christianity. My three children and I spent every possible minute doing what I thought was God's work. We tried to make people aware that there is a devil, and that demons do exist—and that the end of the world was very imminent. I believed sincerely all the concepts taught me by the Jehovah's Witnesses because they were scriptural. We were also told that devils and demons would harass us and try to make us turn away from Jehovah God. I was careful to follow closely to scriptural teachings in order to avoid assault by demonic forces.

"My husband had always been a heavy drinker and eventually became a full-blown alcoholic. He was rarely home at night and when he did come in, his breath would reek of liquor and cigarettes. My husband worked at a factory where he got smelly and dirty. He rarely bathed or shaved.

"Sexual intercourse with him became undesirable and eventually abhorrent to me. I avoided physical contact, in a passive way. The teachings were— no matter how bad a man is, he's still greater than a woman. A woman is considered a 'lesser vessel,' and is told that she is to be obedient to her husband 'as unto God,' in fundamentalist sects. Adultery, of course, is unpardonable and unthinkable. Resistance to any demand a husband might make would be considered a sin before God.

"Desire or lust is also an unconscionable sin in fundamentalism. But my young body didn't seem to understand. I began to have very realistic sexual dreams in the morning after my husband went to work. One morning I actually came to full orgasm for the first time in my life during the amorous attention of my dream lover. I awoke from the dream with my entire body responding and throbbing rhythmically to the thrusts of my more than adequate spirit lover.

"Being totally out of control from reaching an orgasm revolted me. I had read sex manuals that said women didn't have sexual dreams. Yet, I was having one almost every morning. My dreams became so real that my lover began to take on a personality. He became more insistent—more passionate each time he took me.

"At first, I told myself it didn't count, but as the assaults grew more real and my own pleasure more pronounced, strong guilt feeling developed. Purposefully, I avoided sleep at hours I knew he'd come to me. It worked for a while but late one night with my husband lying beside me, a light touch awakened me. I opened my eyes and saw a dark form by my side reaching toward me. Thinking a robber had entered the house, I screamed. My husband woke up in time to see the dark silhouette of a man disappear into a closet. He took the pistol from the nightstand, searched the closet and the whole house —no one was present. We were both mystified.

"The following morning before my husband awoke for work, I thought one of my children had come into the room. They would do that when a storm or noise would frighten them. I'd take them to bed with us until they'd fall asleep, then carry the sleeping child to its own bedroom. I brushed the sleep from my eyes. But instead of a child being in the room, it was the dark man again. This time I knew he was no stranger. My body responded to his presence and he knew it. I was wide awake sitting up in bed, with my husband lying asleep beside me, and my whole body was aching to receive the embrace of the shadowy stranger. As his arms slipped around me, in the darkness, his mouth closed over my lips. Yet I couldn't discern features, just feelings. Gently, he lowered me onto the bed and pressed his body against mine. My body trembled in excitement waiting for him to penetrate me, but suddenly

I came to my senses—in time to realize that I was not dreaming but about to be made love to by a phantom lover, a dead thing from another dimension. Or, at the very worst, the devil or one of his angels.

"I resisted. My struggle and screams awakened my husband. My demon lover released me with a sigh, and once again both my husband and I saw the form of a man standing in front of us and he just disappeared.

"Shortly thereafter, I decided to divorce my husband. My former religious teachings are that the only grounds for divorce is adultery. If adultery can't be conclusively proven, then a divorce is not recognized by the organization and the divorced person becomes an outcast and is not allowed to remarry. Adultery is very hard to prove and in my case, impossible. When I left my religion behind and my alcoholic husband, the dark stranger never came to me in the night again. But I also discovered that no mortal man could ever be his equal as a lover.

L. L.
Florida"

In the instances that you've just read, it appears that entities are most adept at the art of lovemaking. It's possible that one reason they are thought to be such superior lovers is that they are beyond human hang-ups, everyday problems and moral guilt. They apparently have but one goal in life, or rather in death, and that is pleasure.

Tread lightly, she is near
Under the snow,
Speak gently, she can hear
The daisies grow.
Oscar Wilde

6

Ghostly Greetings
From The Graveyard

When I was a small boy, I remember seeing a movie that opened with the scene of a graveyard in Transylvania. I believe it was *The Son of Frankenstein.* Igor, Dr. Frankenstein's hunchbacked assistant, was creeping through the cemetery one night in quest of spare parts for the doctor's ailing monster. Suddenly, the misshapen little man let out a cry of terror. His coat had become snarled on a skeletal hand protruding from a partially opened grave. With a frightened look on his face, he tore loose from the grasping claw-like fingers and hobbled off amongst the gnarled trees and toppling tombstones.

Hollywood created the idea of what a graveyard looks like—one in which the dwellers have returned from the dead. However, when I visited a number of so-called haunted cemeteries while preparing this book, I found them to be mostly peaceful and tranquil habitats for the deceased. In fact, some resembled garden-like parks rather than repositories for the dead. Around the turn of the century, big-city cemeteries were even a favorite place for Sunday picnics. Graveyards are really not the spooky places that Hollywood directors would have us believe—at least during the daylight hours.

When General Felix Agnus, publisher of *The Baltimore American,* died in the 1920's, his family had him interred in Pikeville's Druid Ridge Cemetery, just outside Baltimore. On his grave they placed a strange statue, a small black angel that perched atop the general's tombstone. The statue's sculptor, August St. Gardens, the premier American sculptor at the turn of the century, called her *Grief.*

By daylight she was a majestic monument to the mystery of the world beyond. But for those beings who fell under her uncanny stare after darkness had descended on the cemetery, she was called "Black Aggie." To them she was a symbol of terror. Thus, Black Aggie became legendary enough to provide periodic copy for the local newspapers, for where else did there exist a statue with eyes that glowed fiery red at the stroke of midnight?

The legend grew. As her eyes glowed in the darkness, the spirits of departed souls rose from their tombs and gathered around her. As the legend goes, living persons who returned her gaze were struck blind. Pregnant women who passed under her shadow—where incidentally, no grass ever grew—suffered miscarriages.

A local college fraternity, still as the legend goes, thought it would be a lark to utilize Black Aggie in their initiation rites. A candidate for membership was ordered to spend the night sitting in Aggie's cold embrace. At the stroke of midnight the cemetery's watchman heard a scream pierce the night's stillness. When he reached General Agnus' grave site, he found the young man lying dead at the foot of the statue . . . The cause of death—fright. Just another ghost story that grew in proportion to the passing years, you may perhaps say. Well, maybe, and then again maybe not.

One morning in 1962, a watchman discovered that

one of Aggie's arms had been cut off during the night. The missing arm was later found in the trunk of a sheet-metal-worker's car, along with a saw. The suspect told the judge that Black Aggie had cut off her own arm in a fit of grief and given it to him. Apparently, the judge did not believe in the supernatural, for he sent the tinsmith to jail.

However, a number of other persons did believe the tinsmith's story. Almost every night, groups of people trekked through Druid Ridge Cemetery, for Aggie became a popular nighttime attraction.

By 1967, things got so bad that Agnus' descendants had the statue removed. It would make a fine cultural donation, they thought. Aggie was given to the Smithsonian Institution in Washington.

Today, Aggie sits enshrouded with cobwebs in the corner of a dusty storeroom. The Smithsonian people never have and probably never will exhibit the statue. Why? "Maybe—just maybe," as Mike Himowitz of the *Baltimore Sun* said, "they're not taking any chances."

There is another interesting cemetery in Baltimore, though many people are unaware of its existence. It is the old Western Burial Ground which houses the remains of such notables as Edgar Allan Poe, Francis Scott Key's son, President James Buchanan's grandfather, five Baltimore mayors—including James Calhoun, Baltimore's first mayor, and fifteen generals from the Revolutionary War and the War of 1812.

The acre-and-a-half graveyard may not be too easy to find, for the Westminster Presbyterian Church, a nineteenth-century structure at Greene and Fayette streets, was built over the cemetery which dates back a century earlier. However, part of the old graveyard is still accessible via the catacombs under the church. And it is in this subterranean cemetery where the ghost of a young girl has been seen lurking near the tomb of Edgar Allan Poe.

During the wee hours on the morning of August

7, 1976, a group of ten ghost hunters prowled the catacombs in search of the ghost. Robert Thompson, head of the spiritual investigation and leader of a drive to restore the old graveyard, said of the search, "No, we didn't see anything, but we sure heard things—like footsteps. It scared the heck out of me is what it did."

Not only do the catacombs hold crypts, some of whose occupants are partially disentombed, but there is also a room beneath the church in which, between the years 1890 and 1920, a number of persons committed suicide.

The place became bizarre enough to entice many morbidly curious persons to express a desire to explore the tunnels. As a result, each Sunday at two o'clock in the afternoon, guided tours are conducted through the sepulcher.

In Los Angeles most major motion-picture studios overlook a cemetery. For example, Paramount backs Hollywood Memorial Park. The Disney studio overlooks Hollywood Hills Cemetery.

Forest Lawn, in Glendale, is often referred to as "The Disneyland of the Dead." It attracts over a million visitors a year. On three hundred acres, more than 200,000 grave sites are divided into sections with names like Vale of Hope, Eternal Love, Ascending Dawn, Everlasting Peace, Sanctuary of Trust and other placid-sounding designations that impress and soothe the living.

There are no tombstones at Forest Lawn, as in most other cemeteries, each vying to outdo the last one. The graves and mausoleum crypts of everyone are marked only by bronze nameplates. Its interrees include Clark Gable, Spencer Tracy, Errol Flynn, Ed Wynn, Humphrey Bogart, Jean Harlow and other Hollywood greats who have crossed the line. Forest Lawn, which claims the largest celebrity population, takes great care to protect the decedents' privacy.

According to popular belief, Walt Disney's body

is being preserved in liquid nitrogen in hopes of being revived one day. However, Disney officials swear that their late boss' ashes are entombed at Forest Lawn. There is a spot under a large shade tree near the Freedom Mausoleum bearing a plaque reading "WALTER ELIAS DISNEY." But, for some strange reason, it is the only marker in the cemetery that has no dates on it.

If you are a graveyard groupie who doesn't want to spend days seeking out the tombs of famous celebrities, then Hollywood Memorial Park Cemetery is the place for you (to visit). Their celebrity list includes Douglas Fairbanks, Sr. (whose majestic grave site alone is worth the trip), Rudolph Valentino, Tyrone Power, Cecil B. DeMille, Marion Davies and Clifton Webb, among others.

Hollywood Memorial believes that its great ones are still entitled to publicity in death, the same as they were in life. The park even goes so far as to hand out maps showing directions to celebrity burial sites. And if you stay after dark and play your cards right, you might even be able to get your Hollywood Memorial Park map autographed. Clifton Webb has been lauded as Hollywood's most famous ghost. He supposedly divides his haunting time between his old house and the cemetery. He and other, unidentified apparitions have reportedly been seen drifting around the park. So don't forget to have your map autographed.

There is a spirit roaming through another cemetery—a spirit that has yet to be refuted. Chicago's Resurrection Cemetery is the haunt of "Resurrection Mary." Her reputation has been known on that city's South side for a number of years. Mary is described as young, blonde, beautiful and always attired in a white party dress that dates from the 1920's or 1930's.

In the beginning, Resurrection Mary was seen only on rare occasions. However, with time, she became more bold. Eventually, she began leaving the confines of the graveyard. She began to watch for passing cars driven by lone young men. Now, when she sights one, Mary jumps into the vehicle, uninvited, gives the driver a story about needing a ride home and guides the driver past the gates of Resurrection Cemetery. Sometimes she keynotes her parting with a kiss. Those who've felt her kiss claim that her lips are "as warm as if she were alive." Leaving the car—sometimes opening the door, other times not bothering with that formality—she walks directly through the wrought-iron gates without opening them, enters the cemetery and fades away.

On occasion Resurrection Mary leaves more than just visual impressions—as shown in a UPI news photo released in December 1977. One night a passing motorist noticed a young girl dressed in white holding on to the graveyard's gate from the inside. Thinking that she had been locked in when the place closed earlier, he notified the police.

By the time a patrol car arrived, the girl on the gate was gone. The officer shined his spotlight through the bars and saw nothing. He called out and received no response. Then the beam of the policeman's light fell on the bars of the gate where the witness said he saw the girl standing. Two of the iron bars were spread apart. The policeman also noticed at the spot of each bend a small handprint seemingly imbedded in the metal.

It is said that New Orleans cab drivers avoid that city's St. Louis Cemetery #1 whenever possible. For there, too, as in Chicago's Resurrection Cemetery, prowls a woman in white. One night a cabbie was hailed by her. He stopped and took her to the address she gave him.

When they got there, she asked the cabbie to go to the door and inquire for a man who lived there. The man himself came to the door, and the driver told him of the female passenger waiting in the taxi. When the man was told what she looked like, he exclaimed, "That's my wife—she's been dead for years!"

The two men ran down to the car. The vehicle was empty. Widower and driver both fainted. Taxi-cab drivers no longer pick up women hailing them in front of the cemetery at night.

Another rendering of a girl-hitchhiker story concerns two Baltimore City College seniors driving along Route 40 East enroute to a dance. They picked up an attractive blonde girl standing on a corner. She was attired in a blue cocktail dress. They invited her to the dance, and she accepted. Everyone at the ball found her most charming. After the dance the boys offered to drive her home and she again accepted, for it was a cold night. One of the fellows lent her his coat, and they drove her home. The next day they returned to her home for the coat. An elderly woman answered the door. She couldn't figure out what they were talking about. After the boys described the girl, she told them that the girl had been dead for ten years. The horrified youths didn't believe the woman. Both the name of the girl they took to the dance and that of the dead girl were the same. The woman told them where to find the grave of the dead girl in a cemetery a half mile away. They found the stone with the girl's name on it. Folded neatly in front of the marker was the borrowed coat.

Sometimes a hitchhiking young girl is picked up near a bridge. When her benefactor gets her to where she wants to go, he goes to the door on her instructions, only to be told that, many years before, she was in a car that crashed off the bridge into the river below. Some versions have her committing suicide from the same bridge. And she's always vanished when the driver returns to the car.

The outer wall of New Orleans' St. Louis Cemetery #1 is actually the back for adjacent rows of aged crypts. Tombstones, hardly any two of which are alike, stand and lean at a variety of angles, while mausoleum structures tower several stories above the gray and white monuments. A number of crypts show evidence of having been broken open by grave robbers. Statuary varies from an angel of death kneeling atop a crypt to a weather-worn unidentifiable figure looking down at the sepulcher on which he stands. It is not too difficult to become disoriented during daylight in that necropolis. At night the situation could become a charnel nightmare.

The crypt marked "Laveau-Glapion" is perhaps the most interesting. For in this tomb are supposed to rest the remains of Marie Laveau. She has been seen floating around the cemetery and also near a cottage at 1020 St. Ann Street, where she was the "Hoodoo" (local variant of "Voodoo") Queen of New Orleans back in the early 1800's. Because of strange rites carried on at her cottage, the Madame's vibes are said to still be present.

From the number of marks scrawled on the face of Madame Laveau's crypt, and the gifts of flowers and prayer candles left each day in front of it, it's obvious that more than a few people believe she is still among us. But whether the crosses, X's and other symbols written on the crypt brought the inscribers good luck, I do not know.

Madame Marie Laveau was born in New Orleans around 1794. Her lineage was a mixture of Indian, Negro and white. Her wild dancing and pagan practices drove fear into the hearts of those who witnessed them. Not only was she known as the Hoodoo Queen, she was also a notorious whorehouse madam. She virtually ran the French Quarter. The great Marquis de Lafayette traveled to New Orleans just to visit with Madame Laveau. Lafayette was himself a student of the occult and was into Black Snake Power, a derivation of Voodoo.

There were actually three Madame Marie Laveaus who reigned over New Orleans' world of Voodoo and similar occult practices. In addition to the one described above, there was also a Madame Laveau who was active during the 1880's, and still another in the 1920's. But it was the first Madame Laveau who reigned supreme over the Vieux Carr'e, with her own network of spies and paid-off politicians. She was the greatest of all Voodoo queens.

The Madame's crypt is not indicative of the power she once wielded. It measures about eight feet tall and maybe half that in width. Its length will accommodate a seven-feet-tall corpse. She shares her crypt with many of her family. Her crypt differs from the other mausoleums only in that it is one of the better maintained. It is not fancy or ornate, but it seethes with energy.

There is a story concerning three young men who paid a companion thirty dollars to spend the night in St. Louis Cemetery #1, next to the tombstone of Hoodoo Queen Marie Laveau. He was instructed to take a hammer and a nail with him.

"What for?" asked the companion.

"To prove that you've been there, we want you to drive the nail into her tomb."

Shortly after dark, the trio escorted their companion to the cemetery gate. They gave him the hammer and nail. He climbed the wall and sneaked off among the tombs.

The next morning at dawn the trio waited by the gate for their friend. But there was no sign of him. By the time the caretaker arrived, he still hadn't shown up. When the gate was opened, the three men rushed to Madame Laveau's tomb.

At the base of her crypt they found their friend—dead. He had made it to the tomb and driven the nail into it as instructed. Something had apparently startled him, and as he jumped up in terror and tried to run, he felt something or someone holding onto his coat, thus promoting a heart attack. He had driven the nail not only into the crypt but also right through his coat!

Throughout our trips researching for this book, we heard various versions of the "nail in the night" story. The incident is also said to have taken place in the belfry of the strange Aquia Church in Virginia. A haunted house on a college campus in Spokane, Washington, is likewise supposed to have been the scene of such a tragic accident.

Both the Aquia Church and its adjoining graveyard are quite haunted. The red brick church stands on a wooded hill overlooking the town of Stafford, which is on U.S. Highway 1 about twenty miles north of Fredericksburg. Over the main entrance on the church's south side, one can read the words: "Built in 1751. Destroyed by fire in 1751. Rebuilt A.D. 1757 by Mourning Richard, Undertaker, and William Copein, Mason."

For well over two hundred years, this beautifully rustic church has in its quiet location withstood the turmoil in the tides of history—the American Revolution, the War of 1812 and the Civil War. Inside, it has one of the only two known triple-deck pulpits. The square pews display the wear from many generations of parishioners, most of whom were apparently aware that something unusual was going on there at night. In fact, after the sun went down, not only did they remain outside the church, they dared not even venture near the adjacent graveyard.

The haunting of the church includes the sound of feet running up and down the stairs, heavy noises of a struggle and the apparition of a terrified young woman standing at one of the windows. The apparition supposedly stems from the murder by highwaymen of a young woman in the chapel during the American Revolution. As the church was not used much during that war, the body was not discovered until only its skeletal remains were left.

Until early in this century, when a new cement floor was laid, the bloodstains where the woman was slain were clearly visible.

A number of gravestones carry skulls and cross-bones. To the modern observer the symbol seems ominous, but the skull and crossbones actually represents an old English burial style that was supposed to remind future generations of their own mortality.

On our visit, as we strolled about the cemetery, Nancy called out to me, "Hey, night people have been here." I walked over to where she was. A sign that read, "AQUIA CHURCH" had been vandalized and sprayed with red paint the night before. Not far from the signpost was a half-full can of red aerosol paint. Obviously, someone or something must have frightened the vandals off before they completed their handiwork.

As we were pondering the red paint, a car drove up. Its driver identified himself as Robert L. Frazier, the Aquia caretaker. At first he was reluctant to talk with us, especially about ghosts and hauntings. But when we mentioned Susie Hallberg, the director of the Visitor's Center at Fredericksburg, and how cooperative she was in our research, Mr. Frazier became more cordial.

He told us about the history of the church and the fact that many folks in Stafford County believe it to be haunted. "When I was a boy, my daddy told me it was haunted. His daddy before him had told him, too."

Turning toward the church building, I said, "Mr. Frazier, would you be afraid to spend a night here, or even go inside the church at night?"

"No," he said, "I wouldn't be afraid at all."

Then I asked, "Have you ever been in there at night?"

He didn't appear nervous, but I could tell by the way he shifted his weight on the tombstone upon which he was leaning that the question had some effect. His answer was a curt "No."

"Do you believe in ghosts?" I asked.

"I do," he replied, "but I never run from anything. I never stayed in the church, but I would. There's a lot of people who come up here, and they see things and take off."

Nancy asked if many people had seen ghosts or things around the church and Frazier said, "That girl down there who works in the filling station won't even come up here."

"But you're not scared?"

"No, the only thing I'm scared of is the people I know, the real people."

"Have you, Mr. Frazier, seen anything up here?" I went on.

"We've seen things up here—me and my son. We've seen them. They look kind of blurred and funny."

"How many times have you seen ghosts up here?"

"I've seen them three or four times, maybe more."

"You keep saying 'them.' Are there more than one?"

He folded his arms and placed them on the tombstone. "I saw two at a time, one goin' one way, and one goin' the other."

Setting the tape recorder on the gravestone, I asked him, "Other people who've said they've seen things up here, was what they saw any different than what you saw?"

"Oh, no, just kinda white figures movin' among the tombstones."

"Were they transparent?"

"No, you couldn't see through 'em. They were just white and blurry-like."

"Are they always seen in the same place?"

Gesturing with an outstretched arm, he said, "No, not all the time. One night we saw them over here. Another night they're over there. When I see something like that, I want to go up and see what it is. But I get up there and they just disappear."

"You said 'we.' Who's 'we'?"

"My boy. My boy and I. Name's Bob jus' like mine."

I continued, "How close can you get to them before they disappear?"

"You can go from here to that fence there," he answered, "about twenty feet."

"When it vanishes," I asked, "does it just disintegrate or does it fade away?"

Straightening up from the monument that he was leaning on, the caretaker said, "It just fades away—kinda slow-like."

"You say they move around. Do they walk right through the tombstones or do they go around them?"

"Around them. One day I saw someone sittin' right there by that cross, and when I got over there they were gone."

"Does it look like a woman or a man?"

"Can't tell. Jus' a white blurry thing. Everybody says there's ghosts up here. Me and my son seen 'em. They're here!"

The ghost in man and the ghost that once was man
Are calling to each other in a dawn
Stranger than earth has ever seen.

Alfred Lord Tennyson

7

The Phantoms of Virginia

Fredericksburg, Virginia, claims to be "America's Most Historic City." Its historical claim may not be accurate, but colonial Fredericksburg may be the nation's most *haunted* city for its size. Virginia is challenged only by Louisiana as "America's Most Haunted State!"

A psychic researcher could spend endless weeks tracking down rumors, and documenting reports of ghostly occurrences in and near Fredericksburg. But such time-consuming effort is not necessary. The Visitor's Center, directed by Mrs. Susie W. Hallberg and founded by the City of Fredericksburg, is a treasury of information for history buffs and investigators of the paranormal alike.

Nearly every building in Fredericksburg boasts an apparition or two. The townspeople no longer attempt to refute their ghosts. They have learned to co-exist with them. And they will not hesitate to speak of such controversial topics as ancestral ghosts and spirit-return with friendly strangers.

The Old South is still alive in the New South, and its inhabitants rekindle those memories and traditions when they spin yarns of family phantoms. Virginians talk about their ghosts as we would speak of old friends.

Little wonder that the shadow of history's greats roam its battlefields and streets, for in Fredericksburg they lived, fought—and died. George Washington was a child here. Commodore John Paul Jones, James Monroe, Mary Washington, the mother of George Washington, and countless other famous persons had homes here. Many houses have been restored. Others are preserved virtually unchanged since colonial times. Is it so unusual, then, that many of the local citizens claim to see the departed ones come back to visit the living?

Since his arrival from England in 1673, generations of Francis Thornton's descendants have lived and died on a vast plantation near the outskirts of Fredericksburg. The Rappahannock River, named for a fiercely noble Indian tribe that once roamed its banks, flows wild and untamed through the land that now embraces the mortal remains of a beloved Indian maiden.

Small, dark and lithesome, the Indian maiden, Katina—a captive slave—moved with grace and dignity among children born to the Thornton household. Yet, she was much more than a mere servant. Katina was the essence of dedication and devotion to the young ones she loved and raised. She taught them the way of the Indian and nature's deepest secrets. Katina died to this physical world but she never left it in spirit. She remains. Her purpose is to see to the well-being of the heirs of Fall Hill Plantation.

Majestic Fall Hill overlooks the torturous rapids and falls of the Rappahannock River and beyond, to a view that extends into the unblemished, pristine countryside. There was never a need to "restore" the old colonial mansion. Throughout the centuries, it remained relatively intact. Today it is very much the same as it was before the Civil War.

Mrs. Lynn Butler Franklin, mistress of the estate,

weaves an enchanting story of a haunting—the spirit return of the Indian maiden known as Katina:

"My grandfather was here when I came to live at Fall Hill Plantation at the age of nine years," she said. "He took me by the hand one day and told me, quite solemnly, 'I'm going to show you the grave of our old family nurse, Katina.' And then he led me to the other side of the farm where there stood an enormous grapevine, as big as a man's body, and three great oak trees. There, we knelt beside a little grave covered by a granite stone. But nothing was written on it. Katina was a slave and the family was very careful not to discriminate or show partiality by engraving her stone. He said, 'This is Katina's grave. When my great-grandfather lived, she brought him up and taught him to speak Indian. She was a very old woman then. My great-grandfather was nearly seventeen when Katina died. He was inconsolable— he wept and said he'd lost his best friend.'"

Mrs. Butler Franklin continued: "Katina was a Sioux Indian. She was a royal hostage—her people had been driven far away to the West by the white man. She was given to Governor Alexander Spotswood and became domestic help in his household with his other slaves. It is a matter of record that a young Indian buck who became beguiled by Katina's charms was arrested and driven away at her request when he demanded she join him. It was Katina's personal desire to remain with the Spotswoods. She stayed to raise the four Spotswood children. And as grown men and women, they never forgot her. I am a direct lineal descendant of Governor Spotswood's wife. Her name was Butler, also."

"And when did the ghost of the Indian girl Katina enter your life, Mrs. Franklin?" I asked.

"Well," she said, "it was in 1938. My mother had a very nice friend in New York. Alice Dickson was her name. She was a level-headed lady—a journalist.

She originated the *Petite Journal*, a French-language newspaper that became quite famous in the States during the 1920's and '30's. Such an accomplishment was no small feat for a woman in those days.

"Ms. Dickson loved my mother and spent weeks with us at Fall Hill. One afternoon, she was taking a nap upstairs. She awoke around five o'clock and started to get up from her bed when a young boy dressed in knee britches walked through the open door. He had his hair tied back and was attired in Colonial period clothes. Behind him followed a little Indian woman with long black braided hair. Thinking the children of the household had dressed up to amuse her, she said quite politely, 'How do you do?' But they didn't answer—just disappeared! There were no children in the house at the time. She'd seen the ghost of Katina!"

"Who do you think the little boy was?" I asked.

"Why, Francis Thornton, of course," she responded. "He was the only boy among five sisters in that generation, and she loved him especially well!"

"What about your personal experience, Mrs. Franklin?" asked Richard as he quickly changed the cassette in our tape recorder.

"My experience was in that room—in that bed," she said as she pointed past us. "It was the dining area in Katina's day. I was wide awake and sitting up. At the foot of the bed appeared a darkly beautiful face. She just looked at me with her native Indian eyes—she didn't smile, nor did her expression change. She just stared at me with a look of great concern."

"Why do you think she appeared to you at that time?" I asked Mrs. Butler.

"It was a period of considerable stress," she said. "I had my little granddaughter with me. We'd just recently lost her father. It was as if Katina were trying to say, 'Now watch out for that child.' That was nearly eighteen months ago. And I'd never seen a ghost of any description before. I'd never seen

Katina, nor thought I would ever see her, and I wasn't quite convinced that *anyone* had ever seen her. Imagination, you know. But there's no question —I was wide awake and she was real.

"There have also been numerous sightings by others who have stayed in this household. Katina has been most often seen near the top of those stairs. She is always seen walking right through a bedroom wall. We discovered that during the 1800's there were some alterations made in the house. At the spot where she appears to walk through the wall, there is, under the wallpaper, an old sealed-up doorway. It was a second door to that bedroom. I believe it was once the nursery."

"Have you seen her since?" asked Richard.

"No, no, and I don't expect I ever will—ever again," she replied with a wistful expression on her face.

On our departure from Fall Hill, we followed a dirt side road looking for a fallen great oak tree that protected the site of Katina's grave near a creek that leads to the river. We saw several likely sites, but couldn't decide which one was the final resting place of Katina. And perhaps it's just as well. The little Sioux Indian maiden is now a part of the legendary forest that she loved so much in life.

Virginia teems with vibrations of the dead.

Overlooking historic Fredericksburg stands Chatham Manor, a beautiful old Georgian mansion dating from 1768. The "Lady in White," the house's resident ghost, drifts vaporously around its formal gardens.

The Park Service has held public tours at Chatham, also known as the Lacy House, since October 15, 1977. Will Green, a Ranger there, will tell you the stories about the ethereal "Lady in White." She is said to have made a deathbed vow to commemorate a frustrated love affair experienced in her youth by appearing on the anniversary of her death, every seven years.

The White Lady's plans for elopement with a man

her father considered beneath her station were thwarted by none other than General George Washington himself. When she descended a rope ladder from her bedroom window, she expected to be greeted by a lover's kiss. But instead, the errant daughter was confronted by the General, who had been tipped off to her plans by one of his servants. The White Lady was taken to her father who shipped her immediately to England. She was forced to marry a man of her father's choosing by whom she bore ten children. She spent her last days there, pining for her lost love.

June 21, 1981, is the next date when the White Lady is supposed to appear. And you can bet the Park Service employees will be vigilant.

You may also be delighted to discover that President Abraham Lincoln was known to frequent Chatham, as well as Clara Barton and Walt Whitman. George Washington wrote letters of glorious praise about Chatham Manor.

"I have put my legs oftener under your mahogany at Chatham than anywhere else in the world, and have enjoyed your good dinners, good wine, and good company more than any other," he wrote of Chatham.

Chatham Manor was a contribution to the National Park Service made by the late wealthy industrialist and philanthropist, John Lee Pratt, who willed the historic estate to the Park Service when he died in 1975.

Kenmore—an English Georgian-style Colonial mansion, originally owned by General George Washington's brother-in-law, Colonel Fielding Lewis—is haunted. The 226-year-old red and white brick plantation house, which was once part of an 863-acre estate, represents the finest of Fredericksburg's Colonial structures.

Colonel Lewis, Kenmore's ghostly visitant, has been seen walking its dimly lit corridors and rooms as he pours over his ledgers. The Colonel wound up financially bankrupt after spending his personal fortune manufacturing small arms during the American Revolution. He died penniless. Now, he spends his time prowling about Kenmore, turning doorknobs and making his presence known by scraping his feet on its stone steps.

Colonel Lewis has been seen by credible witnesses on several occasions in full Revolutionary period garb, appearing to be going about his daily business. His wife, General George Washington's only sister, Betty Washington, has never been seen at Kenmore.

However, a female specter has been seen in St. George's Church, where Colonel Lewis is thought to be buried under the front steps. And Sir Alexander Spotswood, Virginia's greatest English governor, is said to roam Federal Hill which was once his residence. Over the years, he has been seen attired in hunting clothes and drinking an eggnog.

He tightened his belt, he took a lamp,
Went down the cellar to the webs and damp.
There in the middle of the mouldy floor
He heaved up a slab, he found a door—
And went down to the Devil.

Vachel Lindsay

8

New Orleans— The Most Hosts of Ghosts

Take a hundred of the most enthusiastic ghost hunters and ask them to name America's most haunted city. Most will spring to their feet yelling, "New Orleans!"

Then ask the same group which is New Orleans' most haunted house. The majority will say the Lalurie house at 1140 Royal Street. Others will say the Beauregard house. Some will insist that 1020 St. Ann Street, where Marie Laveau lived, is the most haunted.

When General Pierre Gustave Toutant Beauregard returned home to New Orleans from the Civil War after Lee's surrender at Appomattox, he was, like so many of his compatriots, a poor man. He settled in a house at 1113 Chartres Street in the French Quarter. The General, who was an engineering officer in the United States Army before the Civil War, took a position as chief engineer for a railroad. Later he became associated with a streetcar company. Eventually, he became the supervisor of drawings for the Louisiana Lottery. During this period he wrote three books on the Civil War.

There are no records to suggest that the Chartres Street house was haunted before the General died on February 20, 1893—nor after his death, for a number of years.

Around 1909, the Giaconas, a well-to-do Italian family noted for its gala dinner parties, occupied the house. One night neighbors reported hearing angry shouting and then a series of gunshots. A man, apparently wounded, was seen fleeing the house with a gun in his hand.

When the police arrived, they found three men dead and a fourth critically wounded. The victims were identified as members of the Black Hand (Mafia). Police investigators found that the Giacona family were victims of an attempted extortion plot by the Mafiosa.

When the Giaconas wouldn't pay off, the extortionists came after them with guns. But the family was ready for them—which resulted in the shootings. Several other attempts on the family by the Black Hand also failed.

After several years during which they maintained their home as a virtual fortress, the Giaconas moved on to more peaceful territory.

In 1925, the new owners of the house decided to convert the structure into a macaroni factory. A number of concerned residents of the French Quarter became aroused upon hearing about the planned destruction of the more-than-a-century-old mansion. The Beauregard Memorial Association was formed to raise funds to buy the house. Through its efforts, the General's home was saved and eventually became a residence-museum.

In the years following World War II, various rumors began to surface about the sounds of men in battle coming from the walled-in garden section. The sounds were not those of modern battle but rather of Civil War musketry, bugles and officers shouting orders. Other reports told of small-arms gunfire and men shouting in Italian.

In recent years, however, there have been no accounts of nighttime battles taking place within the walls of the old Beauregard House. According to Alma H. Neal, director of the Beauregard House, on the matter of hauntings, "We do not know of anything supernatural taking place here," she said.

The Lalurie Mansion, considered New Orleans' most haunted house, has a rather bizarre history. However, the history is probably more bizarre than the house itself.

The Lalurie House, a typical French creole mansion, has been the subject of fantastic stories ever since it was built in 1832 as the residence of Dr. Louis Lalurie and his twice-widowed bride.

Madame Delphine Lalurie became renowned for the social affairs that were held in the mansion. A shrewd businesswoman, she was one of the most prominent French-Creole women in New Orleans. Her husband, many years younger than she, had little to do with her business affairs.

Wherever she went about the city, small children would run after her sleek phaeton coach, which was driven by a regally dressed Negro coachman. When enough children were following the coach, she would disperse them by throwing a handful of pennies onto the cobblestone pavement. Her own two daughters were among the finest-dressed young girls in the French Quarter.

This was Madame Delphine Lalurie as seen by the citizenry. But there was another side to the woman that very few people were aware of. In this manifestation, she was a cruel, cold-blooded, almost demonic wench. Behind all of the splendor there was much despair and torment.

In the kitchen, located on the floor below the banquet hall, she kept the cook chained within twenty feet of the fireplace where the sumptuous dinners were prepared. No visitors were ever allowed in the kitchen.

Her neighbors were unsuspecting of the Madame's sadistic maltreatment of her servants. But one afternoon a neighbor was climbing her stairs. Suddenly, she heard a shriek from the Lalurie courtyard. Looking out she saw a little Negro girl, no more than eight years old, fleeing across the yard toward the house with Madame Lalurie in hot pursuit, whip in hand. The lady saw the poor child running from story to story up the Lalurie's back porches until both came out on top of the house.

Observing the child about to leap in terror from the roof, the woman covered her eyes. But she heard the scream of the falling child and heard the body hit the courtyard. Then she watched as the tiny body, nearly every bone broken, was picked up and taken into the house.

After continuing to observe from her own house for many hours, the lady saw the body brought back out after dark and buried in a shallow grave in a corner of the courtyard.

During that period, there was a slave-protection law which ordained that slaves proved to have been cruelly treated would be taken from their owner and sold at public auction for the benefit of the State.

No secret was made of the child's death, and an investigation proved illegal cruelty in the case of nine Lalurie slaves, who were forfeited according to law.

However, the subject slaves ended up again as Madame Lalurie's property, because she induced some relatives to purchase the slaves and sell them back to her. One morning the cook declared that they would all be better off being burned than leading such a miserable life. Then she set the house on fire. Soon most of the mansion was in flames.

After the fire was extinguished, the fire fighters were greeted by a horrible vision of the nine slaves. The skeletons of two were found poked into the ground. The other seven, still alive, were barely recognizable as human beings. Their faces had the wildness of famine, and their bones protruded through their skin. They were chained to the wall in various positions. Around their necks were spiked iron collars. Blood-stained whips hung on the wall. There was a stepladder on which Madame Lalurie must have stood in fiendish ecstasy as she flogged her victims. Each morning after breakfast, it was said, she would lock herself in with her slaves and flog them until her strength failed. Two of the slaves had died in the fire. The rest, maimed and helpless, were placed on city pensions.

When word was spread about the Madame's slaves, enraged townspeople sought her out. But she and her husband, along with the coachman, drove to where a schooner lay alongside the levee. Leaving the slave with the carriage, the Laluries hired the vessel to take them to Mobile, where they caught a ship to France.

The New Orleans mob met the returning carriage, smashed it to pieces and stabbed the horses to death. The coachman barely escaped with his life. The enraged mob moved back to the mansion where they set fire to the undamaged portion. Madame Lalurie's two daughters, whom she had abandoned, managed to flee through a window and went to live with relatives.

Sometime later, Madame Delphine Lalurie was found living in Paris under an assumed name. A group of "gentlemen" called on her one night and told her that she had best be off before dawn. She was never heard from again.

Today, nearly a century and a half later, it is said that if one passes the now restored Lalurie Mansion on certain nights, he or she will hear coming from the courtyard the scream of the Negro child plunging to her death. And from the attic can be heard the groaning of slaves as they rattle their chains in eternal agony.

Back in the 1960's, Mrs. Richards, a visitor at the house on Royal Street, reported numerous poltergeistic activities, such as opened water faucets, locked doors becoming unlocked, and showers turned on by themselves.

Today, none of the several residents of nearby buildings recall ever witnessing any occult occurrences around the old mansion. We can only conclude that the once haunted Lalurie house is no longer haunted, and that its reputation is maintained as a status symbol.

Outside the French Quarter, there is an antebellum mansion at 1447 Constance Street which has been haunted for as far back as anyone in the neighborhood can remember. Yet it has received virtually no publicity.

Actually, the house, built in 1852, is relatively new by New Orleans standards. Its first owners, Mr. and Mrs. Adam Griffon, lived there for only a few years. The next owners had their occupancy cut short by the Civil War.

New Orleans fell very early in the war. When General Ben Butler's Union troops arrived in the city, they began selecting various houses and buildings in which to house men and supplies. The house at 1447 Constance Street was one of them. However, the first soldiers to enter the house heard the rattle of chains and moans of agony coming from upstairs. But they found nothing unusual on the second floor. In the third-floor attic, however, they discovered a scene as grisly as anything they'd seen in combat. One side of the attic was lined with shackled slaves chained to the wall. All were in a state of advanced starvation. Some had gaping, maggot-infested wounds. The slaves were removed to a field hospital, and the house was designated as a barracks for prisoners and soldiers.

Before his troops occupied New Orleans, General Butler issued an order to shoot all looters, including Union soldiers. Two Union officers arrested for looting were confined to the third floor of 1447 Constance Street to await court-martialing. They spent much of their confinement time drinking cheap whiskey given to them by the guards. They kept singing "John Brown's Body" over and over again.

Their repetitious singing of the Union song was really a cover-up. They were actually Confederate deserters who stole the Union uniforms and were wearing them at the time they were caught looting. Knowing that if it were discovered that they were really Southerners, they would be given a quick trial and shot, the pair attempted to throw off suspicion by singing "John Brown's Body."

However, when they learned that all looters, Union or Confederate, would be shot, they bribed a guard to get them a pair of pistols. Then they lay down beside each other on a bed. There, each placed his revolver against the other's heart. Then, apparently, they counted to three and pulled the triggers.

After the Civil War, the building was used almost continuously for commercial purposes—as a lamp factory, a mattress plant, a perfume-bottling company and, during the 1920's, as a hiring hall for a stevedoring firm. Its last occupant before the present owners purchased the house was an old man who rebuilt air conditioners—before he disappeared one day.

Down through the years there have been many reports of two white-faced soldiers wearing blue uniforms standing at a third-floor window, bottles in hand, singing "John Brown's Body." On other occasions the rattling of chains followed by bellowing and screams have been heard.

Another incident occurred during a short period when the building was being used as a rooming house. A widow rented a second-floor room. One afternoon she was sitting at the window looking out on Constance Street when she noticed some blood on her arm. Thinking she might have unknowingly scratched herself, she wiped the blood away. In an instant the blood was back. Before she could wipe it off, she discovered another drop of blood on her arm, and another, and another. Instinctively she looked up. Blood was oozing through a crack in the ceiling directly above where she was sitting. As she fled down the stairs, she heard the strains of men's voices singing "John Brown's Body."

One night when the house was being used as a lamp factory, the Negro maintenance man was working alone. It was shortly before midnight, and he was on the second floor when, before his startled eyes, a door swung open. As he stood there staring in disbelief, a pair of boots—or at least the sound of boots—marched through the door. Then a second pair of boots paraded past the terrified man. No sooner had the sound of the marching boots faded away when he heard the drunken laughter of men, followed by the singing of "John Brown's Body." The song could still be heard by the caretaker as he fled down the stairs and out onto Constance Street.

On another occasion, the factory's two owners arrived to open up one morning. As they entered the building, a huge block of concrete came hurtling down the steps, barely missing the two men. They charged upstairs to find the culprit, but there was no one there. In fact, the floor upstairs had been painted the previous day and was still tacky. Yet, there were no footprints in the fresh paint!

There are stories of people who went into the house as late as twenty years ago who told about secret chambers and finding a chest full of shackles and dried bloodstains. In August 1951, New Orleans was struck by a great hurricane that took two hundred and seventy-five lives. A tide eleven feet above normal swept the area. Damage to property amounted to more than thirteen million dollars. During the storm the old slave quarters behind the house were destroyed. When the debris was being cleaned out, workers discovered a tunnel running beneath the house leading to the street. No one knew the purpose of the passageway. However, an old chest bound with chains was found in it, along with some old uniforms and a quantity of trash.

Kathleen Jones and her husband Anthony now own and are restoring the old house. She said, "We both believe in ghosts, or whatever one chooses to call them. But we can't give any supporting evidence about our house. Many times during our labors we entreated the spirits to return and give us a hand, but they never did."

However, before he vanished, the old man who used to rebuild air conditioners in the house told neighbors that he had "seen things," but he never would elaborate.

A handsome black man who lives across the street, commented, "I know it's haunted."

"What makes you so sure it's haunted?"

He told us this story: "It was just before Christmas of last year [1977]. I drove my car out of the driveway here, and as soon as I was in front of that house, my front tire went flat. This was between ten and eleven at night. You know, I had often wondered why some people cross the street instead of passing in front of that house at night. Well, anyway, while I was mounting the spare wheel, I heard loud laughter coming from the house. Then, suddenly, there was the sound of smashing glass, like someone breaking bottles, coming from inside. The house was dark and empty. The new owners were fixing it up during the day. But at night they stayed somewhere else. I'll never forget how eerie that laughter sounded."

I asked him if he went up on the porch to investigate. His reply was right to the point. "No, I just got the hell out of there."

Across town, just beyond the French Quarter in the Marigny District, is another house that has actually been the scene of apparitions and other strange manifestations. It is an old two-and-a-half-story structure located right off Franklin on Royal Street. The house on Constance Street was written up once a number of years ago. But, to the best of our knowledge, this strange house at 2606 Royal Street has never been mentioned in any writings on the supernatural before.

The one-time occupant, Ramon, is a thirty-year-old man of Creole extraction who was born and raised in New Orleans. He was most delighted to discuss haunted houses with us. "They're always talking about the Lalurie and Laveau houses being so haunted. Those houses are kid stuff compared to the house I used to live in. It was built around 1830. The party who sold it to my grandmother just after World War II only lived there for three years. They sold it cheap because it was haunted. Before that it stood vacant for twenty-five years."

"Did you ever see anything in there?" asked Nancy.

"My sister and I, her name's Teresa, when we were children and misbehaved our mother would punish us by making us sit in the hall on a big hassock at the bottom of the stairs leading to the attic. Well, almost every time we sat there in that dark hallway we'd see this woman we didn't know come walking down the steps.

"She wore a long dark dress with lace and a V-shaped neckline. She had brown eyes and long dark hair. She was very Creole-looking. Sometimes there would be a little white dog with her."

I continued with my questioning. "Both you and your sister saw the ghost. Did anyone else see her?"

"It was a big house with three floors and quite a few rooms," he replied, "and it was right after the war when there was a housing shortage. My family lived there with my grandmother—her name was Pauline Ruez—and my two uncles and their families. We all saw the ghost at one time or another.

"My sister Teresa probably saw her more often than anyone else. She called the ghost 'Mini Canal.' That was when she was quite young, about four or five. My mother kept asking her where she learned that name. Teresa didn't know, but she always referred to the lady on the stairs as 'Mini Canal.' I started calling her that, too, and so did my cousin Alfrien. In fact, one day my cousin was making jokes about 'Mini Canal'—sort of making fun of her. Late that night everyone in the house heard him scream. His mother ran to his bed. He was crying and said that 'Mini Canal' had slapped his face. When they turned the lights on, they saw that the whole side of his face was red.

"Another time, my father was lying in bed and he saw who he thought was my mother. She also had long brown hair. He was about to say something to her when he felt something moving in bed behind him. He turned around and saw that it was my mother, sleeping. When he looked back at the sofa, there was no one there."

The next morning, Ramon and his sister Teresa picked us up at the hotel and we drove to their old house on Royal Street. It was an unprepossessing structure with no front yard, two stories tall plus an attic. On the second floor there were three eighteenth-century French doors. Two large windows facing the street on the ground floor were boarded up. The feeling of antiquity was lessened by a small air conditioner hanging out of the attic window.

After we rang, almost ten minutes passed before anyone answered the front door. When it finally opened, we were greeted by an aspiring ex-New York stage and film producer who had relocated to New Orleans. The dark inside hall was not the most cheerful entryway that I'd ever been in. However, once in the living area, the old building was fixed up quite unlike the way it was when Ramon and his sister lived there. The huge fireplace, in front of which the children used to spend their winter nights, was sealed. Many of the original walls were covered with wood paneling. The winding stairway remains unchanged, except for the paint brushed over the mahogany banister.

"See that little room under the stairs there?" said

Teresa. "An old lady once told us that slaves were kept in chains there."

Resting one hand on the banister, Nancy said, "So these are the stairs the phantom lady walked down when you two were kids!"

"Up there," said Teresa, "is the third-floor level that no one except the children would ever use . . . until my uncle boarded it up to keep us out of it. Sometimes we'd hear a dog bark up there, but when we'd run up the stairs to the attic, we couldn't find any dog.

"My grandmother was the first person to ever see the ghost. She used to sleep in the bedroom on the second balcony landing. One night, she was in there reading the Bible, as she did quite often. She heard my aunt's baby, an infant in a crib, crying and crying. So she came to the end of the stairway, where she saw a lady with long dark hair bending over the crib. My grandmother thought it was my aunt, because we all had long black hair. She shouted to her, 'Rita, don't you hear the baby crying? Rita! Can't you hear the baby?' The figure next to the crib didn't move. After repeating the question again with no response, my grandmother became angry and stomped her foot and shouted, 'Rita!' And when she did, my aunt got out of her bed and went to the doorway where my grandmother stood. Then my grandmother saw this vision leave the cribside and just go through the wall, as if it were trying to hide, and into the closet.

"My aunt said, 'What do you want, Mother?' And Grandmother looked toward the closet and the vision was still there.

"The second sighting of the ghost was made by my mother. There was a phone located on the second stairway in the hall by the attic stairs. She was in the house alone. Everyone had gone outside except me. My mother was pregnant at the time with her second baby. She went up the stairs to call my father to see how late he'd be getting home from work that night. While she was dialing, she heard what sounded like pattering little feet coming down from the attic—the sound of a dog's paws padding down the stairs. When she glanced up she saw a cute little dog, a terrier—a little white terrier. She stared at it and then she saw a lady following behind the dog. As the woman's form came closer to her, it was obvious to my mother that the form was not human. She was so frightened that she dropped the phone. My mother had a religious symbol on a chain around her neck. The only thing she could think to do was to grab the medal and pray. Clutching it, she ran all the way down the stairs, too frightened to look back."

I couldn't help but notice how both Teresa and Ramon kept glancing up the darkened stairway as she talked. It was almost as though they were expecting to see the phantom lady come floating down toward us.

Leaning against the post at the bottom of the banister, Teresa went on with her story:

"My mother was in her seventh month of pregnancy when she was so terribly frightened by the appearance of the lady. Shortly afterward she gave birth to the baby, and it was stillborn.

"A lot of times, after midnight, we could hear moaning sounds like a woman crying coming from the attic. And then my Uncle Santos, who was coming home from work late one night, saw the ghost lady coming down the stairway from the attic toward the end of the balcony. Then she disappeared.

"Another night, when he was climbing up the stairs, he actually had to move aside to let the icy-cold figure pass him on the steps. He was so frightened, he ran into the bedroom and locked the door to protect the children and his wife."

"Except for your cousin's slap in the face," said Nancy, "there's really not too much in the way of malevolence that you can attribute to the ghost. Your mother's stillborn baby could be the result of a number of different things. The ghost slapping your cousin's face could be interpreted as punishment—just as a mother would slap a child for showing disrespect."

"There have been a number of unpleasant things associated with the ghost," said Teresa. "My uncle Louis saw her and died right afterward in a car accident. He was quite young.

"My Uncle Robert never had any emotional problems until he saw the lady. It shook him up whenever he saw her. He tried to commit suicide by cutting his wrists. Once my mother saw him as she walked into the bedroom at the end of the balcony, and got there just in time. He didn't seem to remember why he was trying to take his life—just that he became terribly depressed without reason.

"Some unseen force kept enticing the children up the stairs and into the attic. So my uncle boarded up the entrance.

"As my brother probably told you, my mother used to make me sit in the hall when I misbehaved. She didn't believe in spanking. And that is when I would see the lady. One day my mother heard me talking while I was sitting in the hallway being punished. She came to where I was and asked me who I was talking to. I told her, 'Mini Canal.' She asked, 'Who's Mini Canal?' and I said it was the lady on the stairs. When she asked how I knew her name, I replied that I didn't know.

"One time I was looking through some comic books belonging to my sixteen-year-old cousin. Suddenly I took one and ran to where my mother was and said, 'Look, Mini Canal!' It was a picture of a skull."

By now Teresa was looking more up the stairs than at me as she talked. I asked, "Were there any other evil happenings?"

"See up there near the very top of the stairs? Well, one day I found my brother hanging by one hand on the outside of the railing. He was only a baby and how he got there we couldn't figure out.

"When my brother was only eight months old, I screamed to my mother for help, as he was strangling because he'd fallen from his high chair and was hanging from it by the neck. When my mother freed him I screamed that Mini Canal had tried to hurt my brother. My mother was so frightened she just held him close, but my grandmother was so angry over the many incidents in the house that she picked up the high chair and broke it into pieces.

"Grandmother had the house blessed and enshrined, but Mother had moved out by then. She was too frightened to stay.

"Many years later, my mother saw a television show about Voodoo rituals, in which several references were made to a term that sounded very much like 'Mini Canal.'"

"Right there," said Ramon, "is where a woman hanged herself many years ago. She just put a rope over that beam and the other end around her neck. Then she climbed the rail and jumped. But before she did that, she hanged her dog. They hanged there over the stairwell for a long time before the bodies were found."

"And for some unknown reason your sister, when she was only four years old, started referring to the apparition as 'Mini Canal,'" said Nancy. "And neither your parents nor anyone else knew what it meant?"

Ramon rested both hands on the banister and said, "Just a few years ago, long after we moved from here, I met an old lady who used to live on this block. She said that she can remember the suicide that took place back in the early 1900's in this house, when she was a small child. The woman who killed herself, and her dog, was a great Creole lady named 'Madame Mineurecanal.'"

On the second-floor landing was an old grandfather clock from which the mechanism had been removed. As I was passing it, the door on its front side popped open striking me on the leg.

As we stood there pondering the peculiar way the

door had opened and touched my leg, I suddenly felt as though my left leg was standing in a bucket of ice water. I told the others about it. "Here, put your hand down by my left leg. It's freezing down here. Feel it."

The others took turns feeling the chill in the area around my leg. "It's about twenty degrees colder there," said Ramon.

Nancy moved her outstretched hand around the vicinity. "It's a manifestation of an energy mass. Maybe the exorcism ritual just put the spirit of Madame Mineurecanal into a dormant state. Now, with the return of Teresa and Ramon, the spirit has been provoked to reactivate."

As we exited from the building into the hot, still and humid midsummer New Orleans day, the door slammed violently behind us.

"I wonder if the tenant is annoyed about our ghost hunting. From the way he slammed the door, maybe one of us said something he didn't like," commented Nancy.

I glanced up and knew she was wrong, for I could see the tenant through a second-floor window. It wasn't him but someone—or something—else that slammed the door shut behind us.

> I am looking for the grave of Sinbad too.
> I want to shake his ghost-hand and say,
> "Neither of us died very early, did we?"
>
> Carl Sandburg

9

A Machine To Communicate With The Dead, And A Great Curse

One would be hard put to believe that the man who contributed more to our present way of life than any other one person; the man recognized as one of the greatest "brains" of the last two centuries; the man who showed us the light, went to his grave deeply involved in paranormal communications.

Thomas Alva Edison (1847–1931), the self-taught genius who began experimenting with scientific theories in his basement as a child, always adhered to the philosophy of anything being possible if components with which to build it are available. However, throughout most of his life Edison remained an agnostic. Although he didn't dispute the philosophies of religion, he did not believe in their truth.

Edison explained to a friend, Allan L. Benson, a noted author and 1916 presidential candidate, "The statement that the universe was made by a Creator does not help, because such a supposition immediately makes it necessary to explain what or who made the Creator." His thoughts on religion, life and death were very definite.

According to Benson, Edison believed that overall

intelligence existed in the universe, but not personality. The inventor did not believe that the intelligence out there had any interest at all in man. Edison theorized that every cell in every animal and plant possesses intelligence.

Benson once asked the great scientist where that intelligence came from. Edison answered, "It is drawn from some common source—a reservoir to which it returns after each individual life ends, to be used again and again forever. Intelligence, like energy, is indestructible and immortal.

"Each cell is intelligent, but some are more intelligent than others and develop the ability to do some things that others cannot do. Some of the cells of a tree, for instance, know how to pump water from the earth into its branches, while others conduct the intricate chemical processes involved in the metabolism of the leaf. My stomach," he added, "knows how to make hydrochloric acid. I don't."

What Edison claimed was that when a person dies, the body, drained of all intelligence, decays. The intelligence remains in some sort of limbo until ready for another body. Could it be that our spirit world is composed of disembodied intelligences described by Edison? Is it possible that some of those intelligences prefer to stay on rather than enter a new body?

With Edison's theory, it is easy to see that it would take very little to create a belief in the paranormal. In October 1920 an article appeared in *American Magazine* entitled "Edison Working to Communicate With the Next World." The article was written by B. C. Forbes, who would later found *Forbes* magazine.

A month later *Scientific American* magazine published an interview with Mr. Edison substantiating the great inventor's views of the spirit world and after-life existence. The article read in part: "If our personality survives, then it is perfectly logical and scientific to concede that it retains intellect, memory and other capabilities and information learned on this earth. Thus, if personality and intelligence does exist after death, it's very logical to conclude that those who've left this world would like to communicate with those left behind.

"I am prompted to believe that our intelligence and personality in the hereafter can affect matter. If this is correct reasoning, then, if we can develop an instrument delicate enough as to be activated or manipulated by our personality as it exists in the next life, such an instrument should record something."

Headlines and newspaper articles around the world told of Thomas Edison's machine to contact the dead. Joseph Dunninger, the famous psychic who was a friend of Edison's, stated that the inventor had actually shown him a machine he was working on with which to communicate with the dead.

During this period of Edison's life, there was a considerable amount of correspondence between the inventor and English physicist Sir William Crooke, who developed among other things the vacuum tube from which the master of electricity developed the light bulb. Sir William had been deeply involved in communicating with the dead, and had even produced photographs of ghosts taken during séances. It was these pictures that prompted Edison to state that if entities from the spirit world could be recorded on photographic emulsions, then there existed the possibility that a device with which to communicate verbally with the spirits could be created.

Most of the press stories about Edison's machine for communicating with the dead were skeptically slanted. A barrage of cartoons and jokes on the subject appeared in French newspapers, carrying such comments as a dying person telling the priest who was administering his last rites, "When I arrive, I'll give you a ring." Another showed St. Peter at a telephone switchboard saying, "I'm sorry, but that line is busy."

During the last five years of his life Edison became a strong proponent of life after death. According to his friend Allan Benson, the last utterance attributed to Edison when he died on a Sunday in October 1931, gave a fifty-fifty chance to the possibility that there might be a hereafter with immortality for the individual.

After the great inventor died, three of his workers noted that each of their clocks had stopped simultaneously at 3:24 a.m., the time of his death. In Edison's library a large grandfather clock stopped at 3:27 a.m.

In the years since the inventor's demise, curators at both of the Edison Museums, in Fort Meyers, Florida, and Menlo Park, New Jersey, have searched for components and plans to the machine for communicating with the dead. So far, they have found nothing.

However, ten years after Edison's death, a séance was conducted in New York City during which Thomas Edison made a visit and talked to the participants. These included medium Mary Olson, electrical engineer and spiritualist Harvey C. Gardner and J. Gilbert Wright, a General Electric researcher and the discoverer of putty. Supposedly, Edison's spirit said, "I think it might interest you to see the blueprint of a device I was working on before I entered this world." The inventor told them the names and addresses of three former associates who might have the working drawings of the spirit-communication machine.

The three persons named had organized a society shortly after Edison's death for the purpose of trying out the machine. Wright and Gardner joined the society and, after studying the blueprints, constructed the device. It didn't work.

Through Arthur Ford, the late renowned medium, Wright and Gardner were put in communication with the spirits of Edison and Charles Steinmetz, deceased electrical engineering genius. The spirit voices told them of some technical modifications that were needed. The changes were made, and an attempt was made to reach Edison with the machine. Wright stated later that although they were unable to reach Edison, they did establish communication with Steinmetz.

The research ended in 1959, when Wright died. Volumes of records and notes on the experiments were left by Wright. However, to date, nothing has been done with that information. The present location of the machine is a mystery.

What was it that caused the great inventor to believe in the spirit world? Apparently Edison's visit to a house on Ridge Avenue in Pittsburgh influenced his outlook on life after death.

One day in 1920, while visiting in Pittsburgh, Edison was told of a house on that city's North Side where all sorts of strange things had happened down through the years.

The house is in a neighborhood of old-fashioned brick and frame dwellings, settled mostly by working-class families. Most residents were aware that there was something sinister about the house. Playing children often threw rocks and stones at the redbrick building, but few dared to venture near the evil structure.

Charles Wright Congelier made a small fortune as a carpetbagger in Texas during the years following the Civil War. He also made a lot of enemies. Deciding that his enemies far outnumbered his friends, Congelier disposed of his assets and headed north by river steamer, taking with him his Mexican wife Lyda and a young Indian servant girl named Essie. When the vessel docked at Pittsburgh for coal, Congelier decided that the western Pennsylvania town was as good a place as any in which to settle and build a house.

The new two-story brick and mortar mansion at

1129 Ridge Avenue, a short distance from where the Allegheny and Monongahela rivers meet to form the Ohio River, was the finest house on the block.

During the winter of 1871, as the wind howled outside and snowdrifts built up against the house, Congelier discovered that Essie, the Indian servant girl, desired the warmth of a man's body, and he was the only man in the house. Thus began a relationship that Lyda Congelier was unaware of. However, when three people live together in the same household, it is only a matter of time before a secret between two of them becomes known by the third party.

When the servant girl didn't respond to her call one afternoon, Lyda Congelier went to the girl's room looking for her. As she approached the door, she heard heavy breathing and groaning coming from within. She hurried to the kitchen and grabbed a butcher knife and a meat cleaver. Then, standing next to the door, she brought the cleaver down on the head of the first person to exit—her husband. As the servant girl stood screaming in horror, Lyda stabbed her husband nearly thirty times.

Several days later, a family friend called at the house. He found Lyda Congelier sitting in a rocking chair in front of a big bay window in the living room. As she rocked back and forth, Lyda was singing a child's nursery song. On her lap was a bundle wrapped in a pink blanket. It contained the Indian servant girl's head.

After Lyda was taken away, the house remained vacant for nearly twenty years—during which two generations of neighborhood children sang about an old "battle-ax and her meat-ax."

In 1892, the home was remodeled into an apartment building housing workers from the industrial area growing nearby. But after two years, the house was again vacant; the workers residing in the building kept hearing a woman's voice sobbing and screaming.

The big house stood empty again until 1900, when it was purchased by Dr. Adolph C. Brunrichter.

Keeping to himself, the doctor was rarely seen by his neighbors. Then, on August 12, 1901, the family next door heard a terrifying scream emitting from the Brunrichter residence. When they ran outside to investigate, the neighbors saw a red explosion-like flash shooting through the house. The earth under them trembled, and the sidewalks cracked. Every window in the doctor's house was shattered.

By the time the police and firemen arrived, a crowd was already gathered around the house. It was assumed that the doctor was still inside, for no one had seen him leave. The firemen entered the house and began searching for the doctor. They didn't find him, however. Instead, they discovered a ghastly, stomach-turning scene in one of the upstairs bedrooms. Spread-eagled to a bloodstained bed was the decomposed, naked body of a young woman. Her head was missing.

Further investigation revealed the graves of five more young women in the cellar. From what the investigators could discover, Dr. Brunrichter had been experimenting with severed heads. Apparently, he had been able to keep some alive for short periods after decapitation. There was still no trace of the doctor. A manhunt had produced no results.

Once again the house at 1129 Ridge Avenue stood empty and abandoned. Neighborhood children feared the "haunted house." Only an occasional medium would visit the dwelling. Soon, word spread throughout psychic circles that the house on Pittsburgh's North Side was possessed by a terrible presence.

Among the many mediums who probed the house was Julia Murray, who detected a "horrible presence" when she visited it in 1922. Objects hurled by unseen hands barely missed striking her. She predicted that the "presence" would kill, and would eventually extend out beyond the reaches of the house.

Several blocks away from the house, the Equitable

Gas Company was nearing the completion of a huge natural-gas storage complex. One of the structures was 283 feet in diameter and 208 feet high. It supported a 5,000,000-cubic-foot gas tank—the world's largest.

To cut costs, a number of regular workers were fired and replaced by lower-waged emigrants, most of whom were Italian. A quantity of vacant buildings in the neighborhood were remodeled into quarters for the newly arrived emigrants. The house at 1129 Ridge Avenue was one of those converted.

Although the Italian workers were aware that something was not right at the Ridge Avenue house in which they were quartered, they stayed on. Apparently their foreman told them that some of the American workers whom they replaced were embittered and playing tricks on them. Also, it was an era of general anti-Italian feelings, for the newspapers were full of the Sacco-Vanzetti murder trial. So the Italian workmen assumed that they were being victimized by practical jokers. That is, until several months later.

One evening, fourteen men were seated at the dining table. They had just finished their dinner and were sitting around laughing and consuming large quantities of homemade wine. One of the men noticed that his brother had not returned from carrying some dirty dishes out to the kitchen. Leaving his jocular companions, the man went out to the kitchen to see what was delaying his brother. In the kitchen he found the door to the basement open.

Suddenly, the merriment in the dining room was shattered by a blood-curdling scream from the direction of the kitchen. Rushing to the kitchen, the men saw the basement door still open. Taking a lantern from atop the icebox, several of the men descended the cellar steps into the basement.

Before they reached the bottom, they froze in their tracks, for in the glow of the lamp they saw the man who had left the dining room only a minute earlier hanging from a floor beam. On the floor under him was his brother, a splintered board piercing his chest. Then a force they could feel but not see brushed past them. They could hear its footsteps on the stairs, but saw nothing. The door at the top slammed shut. The men waiting behind in the kitchen saw nothing. But they later reported hearing doors being slammed throughout the house.

When the police arrived, they reflected the prejudice of most of the townsfolk. They attributed both deaths to accident. The first man, they said, tripped on a loose stair tread and fell, impaling himself on the propped-up board. The other brother's death was blamed on the same stair tread which, the police said, made him fall, too, causing his head to become snared by an electric wire that was hanging loose near the stairs.

New York's Bowery is a long way from Pittsburgh's North Side. It is the Mecca for all of the bums, down-and-outers and derelicts of the United States. In September 1927, an old man was found there, wandering around in a drunken stupor. As he was being booked before being thrown in the drunk tank, he gave his name as Adolph Brunrichter. He told of how years earlier, at the turn of the century, he had bought a house in Pittsburgh to which he enticed ten young women as guests. Anticipating romance, the women were instead beheaded and used in experiments to keep severed heads alive. Brunrichter told stories of sex orgies, torture and murder, and of how he came under the demonic spell of one Madame Aenotta. He told of another ten women used for experiments at other locations outside Pittsburgh. The locations of the grave sites were checked, but no bodies were found.

After a month behind bars at Blackwell's Island, the man the newspapers headlined as "The Pittsburgh Spookman" was released. On the wall of his cell, scrawled in blood, was the message, "What Satan hath wrought, let man beware." Nothing was ever heard of again from the man who claimed to be Dr. Adolph Brunrichter.

Two weeks after Brunrichter's release, a catastrophic occurrence took place on Pittsburgh's North Side in the neighborhood of 1129 Ridge Avenue.

On Monday, November 14, 1927, at 8 a.m., a crew of sixteen workers climbed atop the Equitable Gas Company's huge 5,000,000-cubic-foot natural gas storage tank to find and repair a gas leak.

Exactly forty-three minutes later, a great sheet of flame shot a thousand feet skyward as the tank rose into the air like a huge steel balloon. The surrounding air was rife with flying girders, splintered steel and falling bodies. Two of the men who'd been working on top of the tank were thrown against a brick building a hundred feet away where their silhouettes were outlined in blood. Seconds later, another tank, two hundred feet away and holding another 4,000,000 cubic feet of gas, exploded, sending up a second mighty ball of fire.

Then a third tank, only partially full, burst and its contents were added to the cataclysm. Smoke and flames were visible for miles. Windows were shattered, downtown skyscrapers trembled and swayed, water and sewer lines burst, flooding streets, and live electric wires were strewn everywhere. The clear day suddenly became night as clouds of black smoke hung over the streets.

Across the street from the gas company, the Union Paint Company was flattened. Dozens of workers were buried in the rubble of that building. Hundreds of other structures on Pittsburgh's North Side were leveled. Many were crushed like eggshells. Bloody men, women and children ran frantically about the streets.

Battalion Chief Dan Jones of Engine Company #47, the first fire unit to arrive at the scene, described the holocaust: "Great waves of black smoke swept through the streets, and there was a whining noise in the air."

AN EERIE TOUR OF PLACES OFF LIMITS TO THE LIVING

GHOSTS AND WITCHES

When this portrait was unpacked, Gibson McConnaughey of Virginia was surprised to find a charcoal rendering of gray, black and white. Later, the portrait virtually came to life in color. (Richard Winer)

Top: During a seance at the Whaley House in California, a shadowlike apparition appeared at the far wall just beyond the oil lamp. (Adele Webster, Courtesy Whaley House)

Bottom: This picture of a dog and the ghostly shadow behind it was taken at a New Year's Eve party. The authors examined the photo and determined that it had not been tampered with. (Nancy K. Taylor)

Left: The ghosts of Hawaii. When word of John Kennedy's death reached Hawaii, the island chain came to a standstill. That night on Maui, there was a tremendous rumble, followed by a land-slide in the Lao Valley. There was a 50-foot high profile of the late president formed in the lava rock. (Roy S. Okada)

Middle and below: Entrance to the Bell Witch cave in Tennessee. The Bell Witch first entered the lives of John Bell's family in 1817. From all over Tennessee came exorcists, dewitchers and expellers of evil spirits. Today, the Bell Witch has manifested itself on Bill Eden's farm which was once land belonging to John Bell. (Richard Winer)

GHOSTLY GRAVEYARDS

Top: An apparition resembling Clifton Webb, the late actor, has been seen roaming about Los Angeles Hollywood Memorial Park.

Bottom: The graveyard at Aquia Church in Virginia is haunted by the sounds of running feet, loud noises and the apparition of a terrified young woman. (Photos by Richard Winer)

HAUNTED HOUSES / PLACES

Top: New Orleans is America's most haunted city.
There is a dispute, however, as to New Orleans'
most haunted house. Some say it is this house
in the Marigny District, the scene of apparitions
and other strange manifestations.

Bottom: During the Civil War, two soldiers
shot each other to death after a drunken party
on the third floor of this New Orleans house.
Sounds of drunken partying, breaking glass
and strains of "John Brown's Body" are still
heard from the boarded-up attic. On occasion,
blood has dripped from the second floor ceiling.
(Photos by Richard Winer)

Left: Manhattan's most famous haunted house, Clinton Court, was built just before the war of 1812 by New York's first governor, Dewitt Clinton. The structure is situated on what used to be a cemetery for the poor. Frequently, ghosts have been seen prowling the area.

Below: It is behind these walls on Alcatraz Island that night watchmen report hearing clanging sounds, footsteps and screams. (Photos by Richard Winer)

Left: The world's largest haunted house—The former Miami Biltmore Hotel. The ghostly entities within the walls number in the hundreds because of all the trauma which has taken place here.

Below: Five qualified para-psychologists communicated with spiritual entities during a seance at the Miami Biltmore in May 1978. (Photos by Richard Winer)

CURSES

Top: Sarah Winchester, heiress to the
Winchester rifle fortune in 1881, consulted a
medium to alleviate her grief over the death of
her husband and daughter. The medium said:
"There is a curse on your life, resulting from
the terrible weapon the Winchester family created.
Build a house . . . As long as you build, you
will live. Stop and you will die." The Winchester
House in San Jose has approximately 160 rooms.
(Courtesy Winchester Mystery House)

Bottom: From the time film star James Dean bought
this Porsche Spyder in 1955, the car gave off a
feeling of impending doom. The car carried him
to his death in September 1955. Since then,
many people who have come into contact with the
car have met grief, tragedy and even death. (Old Cars)

Even rescue workers were killed and injured as weakened structures collapsed on top of them. Entire districts were flooded with water from broken water mains. Houses, factories, warehouses and industrial plants lay in ruins. Entire streets had been heaved up into the air. Sections of the giant gas reservoir were found a thousand feet away. Many of those who died were killed by falling pieces of steel.

On the following day, the headlines of *The New York Times* read, "TWENTY-FOUR KILLED IN GAS TANK EXPLOSION AT PITTSBURGH. SIX HUNDRED HURT, THIRTEEN MISSING. RUINS DYNAMITED IN SEARCH FOR MORE BODIES."

By the next day, there were twenty-eight dead, six hundred injured and dozens missing. Mobs stood outside the downtown morgue waiting for identification of the unidentified bodies. Others wandered through the streets trying to find where their homes had been.

Mounds of rubble and debris marked where structures had once stood. Only at one place were there no structural remains. At 1129 Ridge Avenue, two blocks away from the blast scene, there was nothing. And although the buildings on either side and across the street from that address were heavily damaged, they were still standing. Yet, where the house of death—the house with the evil presence—once stood, there was nothing. Only an eighty-five-foot-deep hole, seventy-five feet in diameter, marked the site. There was no debris, no wreckage—nothing but a crater.

It is portentous and a thing of state,
That here at midnight in our little town
A mourning figure walks and will not rest,
Near the old courthouse, pacing up and down.

                                        Vachel Lindsay

10

Patriotic Spirits,
Military Ghosts

Very few individuals ever served in the military
without undergoing at least one traumatic experience.
Researchers of the paranormal believe that hauntings
can be a result of some trauma suffered by an
entity when he or she was still in the world of the
living. A number of former and present military bases
have been the sites of apparitional appearances. And
in most instances, there have been no denials by
government officials that the hauntings do occur.

In 1955, the United States frigate *Constellation*
made her last homeward-bound voyage. She returned
to Baltimore where she had been launched one hundred and fifty-eight years previously. She was the
first U.S. Navy ship to defeat an enemy man-of-war
at sea. The frigate was the first American warship
to enter Chinese waters. The *Constellation* is the
oldest ship in the world continuously afloat.* She has
been commissioned and decommissioned more

---

*She is forty-four days older than "Old Ironsides," the
Constitution.

times than any other U.S. Navy ship. The *Constellation* is haunted.

Today the old sailing ship serves as a tourist attraction on downtown Baltimore's waterfront. She is maintained and supported by a non-profit group called The Friends of the Constellation.

From the first day the frigate arrived in Baltimore harbor in the fall of 1955, reports of strange sounds and shapes aboard the vessel were received by Lieutenant Commander Allen Ross Brougham, executive officer at the Baltimore Naval Reserve Center.

An apparition appearing as an officer, probably a captain, dressed in an early 1800's uniform has been seen by a number of persons, including Commander Brougham. "It was all over within the time he took to make a single stride," said Brougham.

At other times, the shuffling sound of running feet has been heard aboard the ship—sounds coming from where there were no visible bodies. A number of witnesses have reported the smell of cordage, or gunpowder, prior to the manifestation.

Sometimes the fleeing figure of a seaman is seen below on the gun deck. It has been suggested that the ghost of the captain is in pursuit of the seaman. Apparently, during one battle, a seaman panicked and ran from his station. The ship's commander chased the young sailor and ran him through with a saber.

Across the harbor from the *Constellation* is Fort McHenry, which flew the flag that inspired Francis Scott Key to write "The Star-Spangled Banner" in 1814. The fort, named after George Washington's secretary, successfully protected Baltimore harbor from the British during the War of 1812.

Today, the forty-three-acre complex, which is designated as a national monument, is operated by the National Park Service. We'd heard stories of strange goings-on at Fort McHenry from as far away as Alcatraz. It appears that throughout the whole

National Park Service, Fort McHenry is reported to be haunted.

Carnell Poole is a supervisory park technician who has been with the Park Service for six years. "It was after my third week of reporting here at Fort McHenry," said the tall, slender ranger. "No one had related any stories to me of spirits or ghosts walking around the fort. One night I was up in my room with the television on, by myself, and I kept hearing noises all during the evening that I couldn't identify. Eventually I fell asleep with the television on. I woke up about two in the morning, and the television was off. Thinking that maybe a fuse had blown or something, I got up to investigate. There was nothing wrong. The set had been turned off with the dial. I do not recall turning it off myself.

"There was another incident about six months after I arrived here, and it occurred about four in the morning. I was awakened by footsteps that were walking along the ramparts. I could hear 'clump, clump, clump,' as though someone was walking back and forth.

"Windows were flying up and going down. I heard a bench being dragged across the brick floor down below. When I went downstairs the next morning, I found the front door, which I had locked and bolted the night before, ajar. Furniture had been moved around."

"What do you call this building where you live and where the events took place?" I asked.

"This is a soldiers' barracks," replied Poole. "The men who were stationed here during the 1814 period would have lived here. It's known as D Building today, but it was Soldiers' Barracks Number One back in 1814."

Shadowy figures have been seen prowling the walls and ramparts of Fort McHenry for as far back as anyone can remember. Some Park Service employees have researched the history of the fort down to the smallest detail. The spirit of Lieutenant Levi Claggert, who was killed at one of the emplacements on the east rampart by British cannon fire in 1814, is believed to prowl the walkways and sally-port area of the fort.

During the Civil War, Fort McHenry was used to house Confederate prisoners. One night a Union soldier on guard duty fell asleep at his post near the main gate. The young soldier was court-martialed and sentenced to be shot. He was confined in the cell house to the left of the sally port as one enters the fort. A friend slipped him a rifle with one bullet. The doomed youth blew his own brains out.

Now it is believed that he pays the price for sleeping on guard—his soul condemned to walk eternal guard duty on the walls of Fort McHenry.

For the 1976 Bicentennial kick-off ceremony, President Ford chose Fort McHenry. The opening celebration was scheduled for early morning, so that it could be carried out by "the dawn's early light."

The night before, rangers and Secret Service personnel made a security check of all the buildings in the fort. As each building was scrutinized, it was locked. Guards were stationed on the walls. Just as they were pulling the two big white doors at the sally port closed, one of the rangers, D. Washington, noticed a shadowy figure in a window of D Building, and pointed it out to the Secret Service men, several of whom also saw the apparition. They went back up with guard dogs but could find no one there. Could the condemned Civil War soldier's spirit have been watching out for President Ford's life?

There are still a number of old forts standing across the United States. Each fort has its own ghost stories. It would be somewhat difficult to determine which bastion has had the most hauntings. But there is little doubt as to which one has the most prominent spiritual hangers-on.

Built in 1609, Fort Monroe in Virginia was

originally called Fort Algernourne. In the beginning, it was garrisoned by English soldiers. Not until 1834 did it bear any resemblance to the fort as it appears today. It had been manned longer than any other Army post in the United States. It is one of only two American forts to have been surrounded by a moat.* It is still maintained by the U.S. Army as an active base. And the Army has yet to officially deny that Fort Monroe is haunted.

Among the V.I.P. ghosts supposedly observed in the fort are General Robert E. Lee, General U. S. Grant (who planned much of his Civil War strategy within the bastion's walls), Chief Black Hawk, Edgar Allan Poe, Captain John Smith of Pocahantas fame, George Washington, Abraham Lincoln and Jefferson Davis, President of the Confederacy. Of these, the apparition of Jefferson Davis reoccurs most frequently.

Although he is remembered primarily as the South's President during President Pierce's administration, he was once an officer in the U.S. Army, Secretary of War, and Senator from Mississippi at the outbreak of hostilities. Jefferson Davis' role in the Civil War is well known.

After the cessation of hostilities, President Davis and his wife Varina started out for Texas where he planned to reestablish the capital of the Confederacy in order to continue the war. It was during the time of this flight that Abraham Lincoln was assassinated. Davis was immediately accused of plotting the President's murder.

On May 10, 1865, a contingent of Northern cavalrymen surrounded a group of tents in a wooded area near Irwinville, Georgia. The officer-in-charge ordered the occupants of the tents to come out with their hands up. As Davis and his wife emerged, he was informed that he had been implicated in the

_____

*Fort Jefferson in the Dry Tortugas was also protected by a moat.

Lincoln assassination plot. The Southern leader immediately denied the accusation and stated, "I would much rather have dealt with President Lincoln than Andrew Johnson."

As a security measure against escape or rescue, the leader of the Confederacy and his wife were put aboard a ship and transported to the country's most invulnerable place of incarceration—Fort Monroe. On May 19, the ship docked at Fort Monroe's Engineer's Wharf, and the first and only President of the Confederacy was hustled ashore and thrown into a casemate cell which was just one step above being a dungeon.

Just before sunset on May 23, officer-of-the-day Captain Jerome Titlow entered Jefferson Davis' solitary cell, followed by a blacksmith and a helper. The blacksmith was carrying a hammer and shackles. Two privates from the Third Pennsylvania Heavy Artillery with fixed bayonets also entered the cell. Two more soldiers were stationed in the guardroom outside the cell. Another pair of guards were stationed just outside the casemate door. Other armed men were posted on the rampart overlooking the area. Across the moat stood another seventy troops— all armed.

Almost apologetically, Captain Titlow said, "Mr. Davis, you are an old soldier, and you know that I have my orders. And I'm sure you know an officer is bound to carry out any order given him." Davis moved nervously about the dungeon-like closure, then rested his left foot on a chair. Thinking that the prisoner was about to submit, the captain said, "All right, Smith, carry out your work."

The blacksmith knelt down to shackle the chains to the prisoner's leg. Suddenly, the Confederate leader hauled off and slugged the man who was holding the chains. The blacksmith leaped to his feet and started for Davis with his upraised hammer. The captain jumped between the two men. It took four men to hold Davis down as the chains were shackled to his legs.

The guard and blacksmith preceded the captain out of the cell. As he was about to step through the door, Titlow turned and looked at the manacled Confederate President. Jefferson Davis was sitting on the edge of his cot, tears streaming down his face.

The orders to chain Davis came down from Edward M. Stanton, who had Davis' former job of Secretary of War. Needless to say, the days that followed were most traumatic for the Confederate chief who once ruled over nine million people.

The incident also took an emotional toll on Varina Davis, who stood at the window of her room for hours on end looking across to where her husband was confined.

The fort's chief medical officer, Lieutenant General John Craven, recommended that the chains be removed. His advice, however, was ignored. But word of the shackling leaked out and reached the newspapers. Public disapproval of the matter aroused so much ire that the War Department ordered Davis unchained.

After four and a half months in solitary, Jefferson Davis was moved to more healthful quarters, through the efforts of Dr. Craven.

Soon public clamor began to demand Davis' release, for no one could offer proof that he had any complicity in the assassination of President Lincoln. Names like Horace Greeley and Thaddeus Stevens —the powerful Republican Senator who championed Negro rights—got behind the effort.

On May 13, 1867, after two years of confinement, Jefferson Davis was released from captivity.

He died in 1889 of bronchial pneumonia at the age of eighty-one. After three days of ceremonies, he was buried in New Orleans. However, four years later his body was exhumed and reinterred in Richmond, Virginia, the former capital of the Confederacy.

Down through the years, numerous apparitions have been sighted in and around the casemate in which Jefferson Davis was confined. Most of the sightings were unidentifiable energy masses of various shapes and forms. They were associated with the Confederate leader because they were seen where he suffered his trying ordeal.

In 1970, there occurred a most unusual happening. Some of the fort's older buildings were being readied for the Officers' Wives Club house tour. In one house just across from the fort's Casemate Museum, some white draperies had been taken down and cleaned. They were returned and laid across a chair until they could be rehung. When the workers returned the next day to put them back up, they found every one of the drapes, even those deep down in the pile, covered with a dusty black soot. The rest of the second-floor room was spotless. There was no way for soot to get into the room, for windows and door had been closed. The Casemate Museum includes that part of the fort where Jefferson Davis was confined in chains.

The windows in the same room would often rattle and shake, especially on windless days and even after they were made tight by wedges jammed behind them.

And it was in that very room that Varina Davis used to spend hours every day standing at the window looking across at the casemate where her husband was being held. She has been seen by many persons in recent years, standing at the second-story window.

One night a woman guest of the fort was sleeping in that room. Early the next morning, just before dawn, she was awakened by a cold chill. As she sat up in bed, she saw a plumpish lady dressed in white standing by the window looking across at the casemate. She got out of bed and walked to the figure in white by the window and put out her hand to touch the stranger. The plump lady simply vanished, and the woman found herself alone and holding onto a white window drapery.

Mrs. Jefferson Davis lived in this room during the period that her husband was held in solitary confinement. What thoughts went through her mind as she stood at the window watching the site of Davis' abuse and degradation? There is no doubt that the experience had a lasting effect on her mental life, making it conceivable that her spirit should recur at that spot.

Before the Civil War, when he was still the U.S. Secretary of War, Jefferson Davis had visited Fort Monroe. He was quartered in the V.I.P. building now referred to as "Old Quarters Number One." On a number of occasions during the Civil War, Abraham Lincoln was also billeted in the same room. It was in those quarters that he spent many hours pondering the tides of the war. That particular room has been named, appropriately, the "Lincoln Room." Apparitions bearing a remarkable likeness to Mr. Lincoln have been observed quite often in the "Old Quarters Number One" building. He has been seen mostly in a dressing robe standing by the fireplace in the Lincoln Room. He appears to be in deep thought.

Of course there have been some other interesting occurrences, too, at Fort Monroe. During the years between the two world wars, the peacetime Army consisted mostly of rough and tumble veterans of long service in the Regular Army. The chaplains' main jobs were not so much to conduct religious services as to get the soldiers to the chapels.

One tough old sergeant stationed at Fort Monroe was Tim Austin, who had nearly thirty years of service in 1933, when he was approached by the base chaplain to attend church. "No, sir," said Sergeant Austin. "If I attended church, the chapel would burn down."

A month later, on Wednesday, April 26, 1933, Tim Austin died of a heart attack on the parade grounds. His funeral was set for the afternoon of April 27.

After the deceased's body was brought into the chapel, the base band, the honor guard and the pall-bearers were seated. The chaplain began his eulogy, telling of the sergeant's devotion to his flag and country. Halfway through the service, someone called, "Fire!" As Austin predicted, the church had caught fire. The chapel was gutted before the fire was brought under control!

Sixty miles up the Hudson River from New York City, standing high on the west bluff, is the majestic-looking U.S. Military Academy. In military circles West Point is rated as the world's leading officers' training school. In psychic circles West Point is also known for its ghosts. Until recently the most famous ghost has been the one haunting the superintendent's house. The one-hundred-and-fifty-year-old spectral inhabitant is described as an iridescent, tall, dark and domineering woman named Molly.

Other ghostly apparitions too have been reported since the Academy was founded over a hundred and seventy-five years ago. Late in 1972, however, a new ghost was discovered. At first, it was thought to be a hoax, but as more reports were made, authorities began to believe that the sightings were authentic. At least, they haven't denied them. The location— Room 4714 in the 47th Division Barracks—was eventually sealed up.

The latest series of apparitional sightings took place in the 47th's barracks in October 1972, when two plebes (freshmen), James O'Connor and Art Victor, reported the strange goings-on. O'Connor was showering when he noticed his bathrobe, which he had hung on a hook, starting to swing back and forth in pendulum fashion. The room's temperature suddenly dropped ten degrees. No windows or doors had been opened.

Two days later, on a Sunday morning, O'Connor saw an apparition in the bathroom. It was a figure about five feet six inches tall, "dressed in a worn full-dress gray coat." It was holding a musket. When the young cadet saw the apparition's "glowing white eyes," he fled the room.

The first encounter in Room 4714 occurred on the following night. Suddenly the temperature dropped and both O'Connor and Victor saw it—"an unclear figure like the silhouette of a man's torso," drifting about halfway between the floor and ceiling. The apparition remained almost ten minutes.

Cadet Captain Keigh W. Bakken and platoon leader Terry Meehan offered to sleep in Room 4714. At 1:45 a.m. Meehan awoke and saw "an image on the ceiling." He awakened Bakken, but the specter was gone. However, both men felt the intense cold that had suddenly permeated the room.

The next night the assistant brigade adjutant, John Feeley, volunteered to share the room with O'Connor. Feeley woke up in the middle of the night and saw the ghost image. He let out a yell that awakened O'Connor. The latter cadet got only a glimpse of the apparition before it vanished. One of the young men placed his hand on the wall where the image appeared—"It felt like a block of ice."

Needless to say, the cadet newspaper, *The Pointer*, was right on top of the story. The next night three cadets on the battalion staff stayed in the room with O'Connor. They had borrowed a thermocouple for measuring instantaneous temperature changes from the Department of Earth, Space and Graphic Sciences. The first remarkable reading measured eighteen degrees Centigrade. Then the temperature quickly returned to normal, twenty-seven degrees Centigrade (a drop from eighty degrees Fahrenheit to forty-five degrees Fahrenheit); the next time it dropped in O'Connor's presence, it registered fourteen degrees Centigrade (fifty-seven degrees Fahrenheit). The cadets carried the thermocouple around the room and discovered that it was always coldest near O'Connor.

On Monday, November 6, two other cadets, Joe Tallman and Gary Newsom, stayed in Room 4714. They experienced nothing supernatural. However, O'Connor spent the night in a second-floor room. He saw the apparition.

Thus, it would appear that the vibrations or wavelengths given off by O'Connor's body might be similar to those given off by the body of the spirit when it was alive. There is no other reason why the cadet would attract the ghost . . . unless possibly O'Connor was mediumistic.

The Pointer speculated on why the ghost would be hanging around the barracks. The building stands quite close to the site of an officer's house that burned down in the mid-1800's. The officer died in the fire. Also, the barracks with the haunted room is located in the vicinity of the graveyard for Execution Hollow.

Since 1972, there have been no further reports of the ghost of the 47th Division Barracks. Whether the restless spirit went away, lies dormant, or if the reports about it have been censored by the Army, is not known.

If the late President John F. Kennedy had not been shot in the back by Lee Harvey Oswald, chances are he might have become one of the nation's greatest leaders of all time. Apparently the *aumakuas*, better known as the "ghosts of Hawaii," along with the gods and goddesses of those islands, realized the greatness of our thirty-fifth President.

Shortly before his murder, President Kennedy visited Honolulu. Hawaiians turned out in hordes to give "aloha" to their most beloved of all presidents. It was the greatest celebration in Hawaii since the end of World War II.

When word of J.F.K.'s tragic death reached

Hawaii, the entire island chain came to a standstill. That night on the Hawaiian island of Maui, there was a tremendous rumble followed by a landslide in the Lao Valley.

The next morning when a road-clearing crew arrived at the site of the slide, they looked up. Not a man spoke for nearly a minute. For they saw that where the mountain had crumbled, there was a nearly perfect fifty-foot-high profile of the late President formed in the lava rock.

Native Hawaiians are devout ancestor worshipers. They believe that when living things die, their *mana*, or energy forces, dissipates. However, when the great chiefs and tribal heroes die, the Hawaiians believe their *mana*, which is stronger and greater than an ordinary man's, remains. Thus, could it be the energy force of *mana* which carved the likeness of the great chief, John F. Kennedy, in a remote valley mountainside? The Hawaiians say the personification was a gift from their great gods and goddesses and the *aumakuas*.

Ancient palaces and castles in Europe abound with the entities of kings, queens, dukes, barons and other royal personages. Even a few jesters, chambermaids and prisoners who died in the dungeons have become haunters. But what about this side of the Atlantic, where leaders have resided in structures that could hardly be called ancient?

The cheerless old structure of 82 Bond Street in Toronto was built by that city's first mayor, William Lyon Mackenzie. He served in the Legislative Assembly of Upper Canada for five terms before he became mayor of Toronto in 1834. During his legislative days he founded a radical anti-government paper that made him a political champion amongst the working classes. In 1861, Mackenzie died in the house on Bond Street.

Isabel Grace, Mackenzie's youngest daughter, married and became the mother of William Lyon Mackenzie King who would one day become Canada's Prime Minister.

Prime Minister King became involved in psychical phenomena and the occult in 1920, and delved in it continuously until his death in 1950. Most Canadians were unaware of their Prime Minister's interest in the supernatural until after his death. It is more than probable that Mackenzie King's involvement in parapsychology was stimulated by occurrences in the house at 82 Bond Street, which has since become a Canadian National Shrine.

Mr. and Mrs. Charles Edmunds were caretakers of the Mackenzie house between 1956 and 1960. Both of the Edmundses have stated in interviews that the house is haunted. As Mrs. Edmunds told the *Toronto Telegram*: "One night I woke up at midnight to see a lady standing over my bed. She wasn't at the side, but at the head of the bed, leaning over me. There was no room for anyone to stand where she was. The bed is pushed up against the wall. She was hanging down like a shadow, but I could see her clearly."

Although the apparition merely touched Mrs. Edmunds the first time, the second haunting was different: "It was the same, except this time she reached out and hit me. When I awoke in the morning my left eye was black and blue."

Another ghostly visitor to the Mackenzie house was the apparition of a bald-headed man with sidewhiskers, wearing a frock coat. All pictures of William Lyon Mackenzie show him with a full head of hair. Actually, Mackenzie was bald, had sidewhiskers and wore a wig.

Sometimes, the Edmundses heard "thumping footsteps like someone with heavy boots," when they were in the house alone. Yet when they'd look for the source of the sound, they'd find nothing.

One time when the Edmundses' son, his wife and their children were visiting, the grandchildren became terrified when the apparition of the woman appeared and disappeared in front of them.

On a number of occasions, there would be a terrific rumbling noise and the house would actually shake. On exhibit in the basement was Mackenzie's 1800's-vintage printing press. Although it was locked and unused for many years, it was once thought to be the cause of the noise and shakings.

When the Edmundses moved out in April of 1960, Mr. and Mrs. Alex Dobban took over the caretaking of the Mackenzie house. They, too, heard footsteps and the sounds of the printing press. On another night Mrs. Dobban heard the piano downstairs being played when there was no one else in the house.

Although Archdeacon John Frank of Toronto's Holy Trinity Church performed an ancient exorcism rite in the house, visitors to the Mackenzie house have said that things still are not all right in the building. Unusual happenings continue to occur.

Sometimes, when Abraham Lincoln's spirit is not materializing at Fort Monroe, he is making his presence known in the White House. During his later years, Lincoln was deeply interested in parapsychology and even had séances at the White House. Eleanor Roosevelt, it is said, had something of a rapport with Mr. Lincoln's ghost.

Harry Truman noted in his diary that "the maids and butlers swear he [Lincoln] has appeared on several occasions." During one instance, when he was continuously disturbed by knockings on his door when no one was at the door, Truman said, "I think it must have been Lincoln's ghost walking the hall."

Norman Vincent Peale told of a well-known actor, whom he declined to name, who spent the night as a guest in the White House. In the early hours of the morning, the actor heard Lincoln's voice calling out for help. When he sat up, he saw "the lanky form of Lincoln prostrate on the floor in prayer, arms outstretched with fingers digging into the carpet."

Whether the White House ghost still prowls the halls and chambers of the residence of the presidents, we cannot say. Mrs. Jimmy Carter refused to comment on the subject.

Both Teddy Roosevelt and Jacqueline Kennedy Onassis felt Abraham Lincoln's presence in the White House. Mrs. Onassis once said, "I used to sit in the Lincoln Room, and I could really feel his strength. I'd sort of be talking to him."

Although Abe Lincoln is the most active ghost in the White House, he is not alone among the entities that prevail there. Abigail Adams, wife of the second president, John Adams, has been seen—usually doing her laundry in the East Room. Dolly Madison has materialized in the White House as well as on the outside grounds. She was especially active during Woodrow Wilson's tenure.

Willie Lincoln, who died in the White House while his father was President, was seen during the administration of President Grant. Then nothing was seen of the boy ghost for years until the Taft administration. There have also been reports about a number of other entities that no one was able to accurately identify with anyone who ever actually lived in the White House.

Why Abraham Lincoln's spirit is so active in the presidential mansion can only be conjectured. Some say that he endured a considerable amount of trauma while serving as President. Others say that the Great Emancipator might be concerned about the current problems that our nation has been facing. Then, too, maybe he just liked being President.

There seems to be a lot of hangers-on in the spirit world of politicians. The Governor's Mansion at Richmond, Virginia, is said to be haunted by a young woman who enjoys looking out of windows.

Another executive mansion popular with the specter set is one located at Dover, Delaware. "I'm torn between being a believer and being frightened," said

Elsie duPont, wife of Governor Pierre duPont IV, governor of Delaware.

Woodburn, as the mansion is called, was built alongside King's Highway in 1790 on land originally deeded by William Penn. It vies with the White House in the number of ghosts known to have chosen it for haunting. There are at least four and possibly as many as six. That's a lot of spectral activists for a structure the size of Woodburn, which is large for a house but small as mansions go. But, then, how much room do haunters require?

Until 1966, Woodburn was a private home. Governor Charles Terry, Jr., was the first head of state to live in the mansion. During a newspaper interview his wife Jessica said to the reporter, "So you've heard about our ghosts? It's such fun to live in a place that's distinguished enough to have legends. In Britain, every house with a history has a ghost or two."

Governor Terry himself once described for newsmen two of the better-known ghosts as "one that rattles chains and one that drinks." The imbibing spirit prefers wine. For many years, as far back as anyone who ever lived in the house can remember, whenever a glass or decanter of wine is left out overnight, most of its contents will have disappeared by morning. One servant swore that he actually saw the ghost—an old man in powdered wig and Colonial attire—sitting at the dining room table slowly sipping wine.

The chain-clanking ghost dates back to pre–Civil War days, when Woodburn was a waystop for an underground railroad that guided runaway slaves to safety north of the Mason-Dixon Line. The fugitives were secreted inside Woodburn to protect them from slave raiders who came up from the South to kidnap escaping slaves and sell them back to their owners.

One night a group of Southern raiders converged on the house, hoping to capture a number of runaways hiding inside. However, Daniel Cowgill, who occupied Woodburn then, and his men drove the raiders off. All fled but one, who hid in the hollow of a large tree. Sometime during the night the Southerner lost his footing in the tree and slipped. Somehow his head became entangled in the slave chains he was carrying, strangling him. He hung there until dawn. Neighborhood children say that on dark nights you can sometimes see the slaver swinging in his chains, from the old poplar tree which still stands. Sometimes he walks the grounds dragging his chains behind him.

On some nights weird moans are heard, especially when the moon is full and the night is cold. They are supposedly the wailing spirits of slaves captured or killed at Woodburn. A small girl wearing a red-checkered dress materializes on rare occasions in the garden, where she appears to be playing. It is said that no one has been able to associate her with the history of the house.

Woodburn served as a hospital for disabled soldiers after the Revolutionary War. A colonel who died at Woodburn during that era still roams the house and grounds.

Is Woodburn still haunted? One night in April 1978, Governor and Mrs. duPont, two of their children, Mrs. duPont's parents and an Associated Press reporter were seated in the living room discussing ghosts and hauntings. The duPonts spend most of their nights at their home in Rockland. But on that night they decided to stay in Woodburn. The reporter was invited to stay over.

Until that night, Mrs. duPont had not experienced anything unusual other than observe a portrait of Ceasar Rodney hanging in the dining room which kept shifting. But things began happening that cold April night.

A gray poodle belonging to Mrs. duPont's mother was locked in a second-floor bedroom. How the dog ended up two floors below in the basement was a mystery. Although no one was smoking any cigars, cigar smoke permeated the house.

A wineglass full of sherry was left on the stairs to tempt the imbibing ghost. By 12:30 a.m. everyone had gone to bed. Around 2:30 a.m. there was the sound of heavy objects crashing down from the roof. An inspection disclosed no one to be outside or on the roof. As everyone was returning to bed, a blood-curdling scream came from the garden area followed by a second scream that seemed to come from the entry hall. Everybody ran downstairs to investigate the screams. They discovered that the wineglass was nearly empty. It is not known whether or not Mrs. duPont is still "torn between being a believer and being frightened."

One of the most written-about haunted houses in New York City is the one called Clinton Court. It has been written about so many times that busloads of curious occult fans have called at the address. On March 31, 1978, we were in the neighborhood of West 46th Street and decided to see if the place was still haunted. It is.

Clinton Court was once a carriage house and stableman's quarters, on the rambling farm estate of New York's first governor, DeWitt Clinton. The structure was built in the years before the War of 1812. Today, Clinton Court is a most difficult place to locate. If you seek out that address, you won't find it on West 46th Street. There is a narrow passageway between two buildings. Access from the street is blocked by a high wrought-iron gate. Looking down the narrow alleyway you can see part of a courtyard. By ringing one of the doorbells, you might get someone on the intercom who will agree to open the gate by remote control from their apartment. If this fails, wait until a likely tenant approaches the gate, greet him or her as though you belong there and walk right on in with the tenant. Nancy and I entered with the garbage man after the manager opened the gate electrically with a buzzer from his apartment.

Except for being completely squeezed out of all space around it by neighboring buildings that abut, the old carriage house has changed very little down through the years. It is three stories tall with outside porches and staircases.

We knocked on a first-floor door to no avail. We climbed the stairs to the second-floor porch. (Only two families lived in the building.) We knocked and were greeted by an attractive young lady named Barbara I. who shares the second and third floors with Trent G. Barbara, who besides her regular job as a television writer is working on a historical novel, invited us in.

The structure supposedly sits almost on what was once a potter's field—a cemetery for the poor. It is not known if Governor Clinton was aware of this when he built his estate on the grounds. Supposedly, a mutineer called "Old Moor" was hanged at the downtown Battery after which the sailor's body was carried to the potter's field and buried. A number of persons claimed through the years to have seen his ghost, but those reports were discounted—until the Danish wife of an English coachman who worked on the Clinton estate saw the apparition.

She fled in terror as he followed her into the house. When she reached the top of the stairs, she turned around to see if "Old Moor" was still behind her. In doing so, she lost her balance and fell down the steps. The fall killed her. And she, too, haunts the governor's carriage house.

Two ghosts prowling the estate became an incentive for children to play "ghost." A little girl named Margaret, who was one of the grandchildren in the Clinton family, would put on old clothes and scare the other children. One day while "spooking" near the head of the stairs, she tripped on the overlong dress she was wearing and tumbled to her doom. After that the other children stopped playing ghost—but not Margaret. For she has been seen many times attired in white.

Other entities in the house are supposedly a sixteen-year-old girl who also fell down the steps, and a British soldier who was executed on the premises.

Trent and Barbara told of numerous poltergeistic activities, such as dishes flying about the kitchen, water from the dog's bowl being poured on top of books and potted plants being knocked off windowsills. The downstairs neighbors have sometimes complained of noisy parties and dancing in Barbara's and Trent's apartments when actually no one was present there.

The sounds of footsteps on the stairs are regular occurrences. One time Trent heard a child's voice coming from the kitchen, along with the sounds of the Pekingese dog playing with someone. When he reached the kitchen to investigate, he found the dog sitting alone, very excited and wagging its tail as though it was playing. Could the Peke have seen something that Trent couldn't see? The dog died shortly afterward. So it is more than likely that the ghost(s) at Clinton Place never left.

Sam Bossard, who has resided in a neighboring building for over eighteen years, told us that he has never seen or heard anything strange or unusual around Clinton Court. However, in the building at 927 West 45th Street, directly behind Clinton Court, Mrs. Jean Taylor and her daughter have heard strange noises coming from outside, but whenever they went to investigate they found no one there.

Do ghosts, spirits, entities, or whatever you choose to call them, have emotions? Quite probably they do. They've slapped living persons, they've played jokes and tricks (poltergeists) on people, they've been heard to laugh and even scream in agony. In fact, if they weren't emotional, would they haunt the places where they encountered traumatic perturbations during their lifetimes?

could look down from the balcony at the ball-room-like thirteenth floor living room and one of the largest stone fireplaces ever built so high in a building. The thirteenth floor didn't always serve as a lodging for the chief however. It also served a more sinister purpose.

"And who are you?" cried one agape,
Shuddering in the gleaming light.
"I know not," said the second shape,
"I only died last night."

Thomás Bailey Aldrich

11

The Island of Tears

Government officials aren't sure how many emigrants entered the United States by way of Ellis Island, but estimates range somewhere between twelve to sixteen million.

Eighty percent of the immigrants were admitted. Those refused entry into the United States were rejected because of illness, fraudulent applications, insufficient funds or because they were believed to have been politically dangerous. Two hundred and twenty-five thousand were turned down because of sickness alone.

It was not unusual for a child to be physically or mentally unqualified for entry. Thus, the parents were torn between returning to the "old country" with the rejected child, or seeing the youngster deported alone. Many children were deported. The steamship company that brought in the immigrant was responsible for the return fare if he or she was rejected. However, parents of a rejected child who were allowed to enter the United States would have to pay their own return fare back to the port from which they sailed, if they wanted to accompany the child back home. Few, if any, had the money to return to their native land. So many had to face the trauma

143

of seeing a child virtually torn from their arms and sent back to their homeland.

If the child was under ten years old, he was sent back in the care of an adult deportee. If the youngster was over ten, he was hustled aboard a ship and sent back alone on his own—destined not for his home village but for his port of embarkation, which could have been hundreds of miles from home and friends. Thus, Ellis Island was often referred to as "The Island of Tears."

When an immigrant ship arrived in New York City, first- and second-class passengers were processed by immigration officials aboard ship immediately after docking and usually allowed immediate entry. Third-class and steerage immigrants were marched down the gangway to a waiting ferryboat or barge, and carried back under the shadow of the Statue of Liberty to Ellis Island.

They debarked onto Ellis Island where, in groups of thirty, they were herded through two big swinging doors and into a dark corridor leading to a long flight of steep stairs.

After being jostled up the steps, they passed through another set of swinging doors into what was the largest room most of them had ever seen. To some it was bigger than the town square back in the "old country." To others, it was even bigger than their entire village. And the number of people in the room was probably more than most had ever seen in one group before.

This room, sometimes referred to as the "Great Hall" and the "Registry Hall," could hold five thousand people and measured two hundred by one hundred feet, with a fifty-six-foot-high arched ceiling.

The vast majority of emigrants who passed through Ellis Island between 1892 and 1954 moved on to a happy new life. There was, however, much sadness resulting from entry denials, separated families, children torn from their mothers and husbands disunited from wives.

Hospital wards were equipped to handle not only those suffering from physical ailments but also from mental breakdowns.

There were approximately three thousand suicides on Ellis Island. These people shot themselves, they hanged themselves, they used poisons and they plunged into the waters of the harbor. Death was prevalent on Ellis Island. Not only was there a large morgue, there was also a crematorium and a bone-crushing machine. The crematory and bone crusher are still there, under the hospital. However, tourists and sightseers are not shown that part of the facility. As you can see, Ellis Island, The Island of Tears, has a bitter past, qualifying it as a haunted place— and it is haunted.

"I don't believe in ghosts, but I heard them," said Dean Garret, former chief ranger at Liberty Island (Statue of Liberty) and Ellis Island, when the latter was first taken over by the National Park Service in 1975. The forty-year-old veteran Park Service ranger spent many hours exploring Ellis Island before it was taken over for public tours.

Garret never believed in ghosts until he visited the island. "I heard the kids. I heard the ghosts of Ellis Island," said the blond-haired man. "I was in the old hospital when I heard the voices. I thought they might be coming from the New Jersey shore a half mile away. But I looked and saw no one on the docks. Then I ran toward the voices which seemed to be coming from the Great Hall. It was empty.

"As I said, I don't really believe in ghosts. But we hear them—the sounds of walking, talking and doors opening in the halls of Ellis Island. When someone reports hearing them," he continued, "we say, 'The immigrants are here.'"

Before Ellis Island officially opened as a tourist attraction, a crew of the federally funded Youth Conservation Corps workers was busily cleaning up and repairing the main buildings. One of the workers,

George DuRan, was walking through a passageway beneath the Great Hall when he heard the shuffling of feet and furniture being moved upstairs. Wondering why the crew was working in the Great Hall, he went up the stairs leading to the huge room. He heard the noise until he was almost to the top of the stairs. Then it suddenly stopped. "As soon as my eyes were level with the Great Hall's floor," said DuRan, "the sounds stopped. I entered the hall and found it empty. There was no one there. In fact, there wasn't even any furniture in the room. I checked later and found out that the rest of the workers had been downstairs all the time. None of them had been in the Great Hall that day at all."

DuRan told of another incident that happened shortly after the island was officially opened to the public. "It was late afternoon. The last ferry had left for the Battery. All the tourists were gone. Each boatload is counted when they arrive and again when they leave. So, I know it couldn't have been a tourist. We were walking through one of the passageways when we heard a woman's voice, with a foreign accent, crying, 'Help me! Help me!' We looked all over, but we couldn't find anyone. It was so confusing that we couldn't even tell which direction the voice was coming from. But it was there."

Martha Blitzer, an attractive technician for the Park Service on Ellis Island, told of voices and the smell of burning candles coming from the Great Hall when it was actually empty. "Then, too," she said, "children's voices crying for their mothers—'Mama, Mama'—have been heard."

A New York newspaper reporter visited Ellis Island in 1978, and he, also, heard the sounds of crying children. Although he was unable to pinpoint their source, he was sure that they were actually the mournful calls of frightened children.

Park Rangers have chased the sounds of the wailing children through the halls, passageways and chambers of the buildings without finding the origin of the heartbreaking sounds.

Ranger Brian Smith said, "You can feel history in here. Sometimes a visitor who passed through here himself, or whose parents came to America here, will break down and weep. It's not uncommon."

When we visited Ellis Island on July 31, 1978, it was a day of steady rain. The dismal rain made the facility look even more bleak than usual. Ms. Blitzer escorted us through catacomb-like passages leading to the yet to be restored buildings. We went down into the semi-dark crematorium, where she showed us the bone-crushing machine. I think that even if it had been a sunny day, there still would have been a feeling of gloominess.

I'm sure that an overnight guest on The Island of Tears, where so many personal tragedies have been forgotten in the pages of history, would no doubt experience an encounter with the spirit world. As Ranger Smith put it, "At sunset, you know, you stand here in the Great Hall, and the light fades through the big windows, and the shadows get longer, and you sort of feel you are standing in America's Haunted House."

> Coming events cast their shadows before.
> Thomas Campbell

12

The Cornstalk Curse

"Of all the Indians, the Shawnees were the most bloody and terrible, holding all other men, Indians as well as Whites, in contempt as warriors in comparison with themselves. This opinion made them more restless and fierce than any other savages; and they boasted that they had killed ten times as many white people, as had any other Indian nation. They were a well formed, active and ingenious people, were assuming and imperious in the presence of others not of their own nation, and were sometimes very cruel." So wrote Captain John Stuart in his *Memoirs of the Indian Wars and Other Occurrences,* in the early nineteenth century.

In 1771, seven nations of Indians—Shawnees, Delawares, Wyandots, Mingos, Miamis, Ottawas, Illinois—and others formed a confederacy that was the most powerful to menace the frontiers of British civilization in the Colonies.

The Shawnees were the most powerful of these tribes. The most powerful of the Shawnees was the famous chieftain Keigh-tugh-gua, which translates to "Cornstalk." In 1774, when the white men were pressing down into the Kanawha and Ohio River valleys, the Indian Confederacy prepared to protect their lands.

The Indians formed a line across the point from the Ohio River to the Kanawha River. The whites

149

and Indians each numbered about twelve hundred men. Chief Cornstalk's voice echoed above the sounds of battle, "Be strong! Be strong!" The broad-shouldered six-foot chieftain led his followers bravely, but they were no match for the white man's musketry. When the Battle of Point Pleasant was over, one hundred and forty whites and at least twice that many Indians lay dead. The Indians retreated westward into what is now Ohio.

A fort was built at the junction of the Kanawha and Ohio rivers to keep the Indians from returning to Virginia.

Cornstalk made peace with the white man. In November 1777, at the instigation of the English, the Indians were massing for a new attack. Cornstalk and his fellow tribesmen didn't want another war, which they would surely lose. On November 7, Cornstalk and Red Hawk, a Delaware Chief, went to the fort to try and negotiate a peace before the battle began. Cornstalk told Captain Arbuckle, who was in command of the garrison, that he was opposed to joining the war on the side of the British, but that all the Indian nation except himself and his tribe were determined to take part in it. However, as Cornstalk put it, he and his tribe would have to run with the stream.

For his peacemaking trouble, Cornstalk, Red Hawk and another Indian were held as hostages in an attempt to prevent the Indians from joining the British.

Cornstalk's name once chilled the heart of every white man on the Virginia frontier, and struck terror into every resident of mountain cabins. His name was associated with several frontier massacres. He was gifted with skills in oratory and statesmanship, he was very brave, and he was a genius in military strategy. (It was Cornstalk's fighting tactics, adopted by the Americans, that led them to defeat the British in a number of battles.)

Colonel Benjamin Wilson, who once heard Chief

Cornstalk speak at a treaty council, said of the Indian leader, "When he arose, he was in no way confused or daunted, but spoke in a distinct voice, without stammering or repetitions, and with peculiar emphasis. His looks while addressing Lord Dunmore [British governor of Virginia* before the Revolution], were truly grave and majestic; yet graceful and attractive. I have heard the first orators in Virginia—Patrick Henry and Richard Henry Lee—but never had I heard one whose powers of delivery surpassed those of Cornstalk."

Cornstalk, and his fellow Indians held as hostages, were well treated and given comfortable quarters. In fact, the chief even assisted his captors in plotting maps of the Ohio River Valley. On November 9, Cornstalk's son, Ellinipsico, came to see his father and he, too, was detained at the fort.

The next day, those in the fort heard gunfire from the direction of the Kanawha River. Investigation showed that two men, Gilmore and Hamilton, who had left the fort to hunt deer, were ambushed by Indian snipers. Hamilton managed to escape, but Gilmore was slain and scalped.

When the bloody corpse was returned to the fort, the soldiers there, in a fit of fury, charged past their protesting officers and forced their way into the building where the Indians were being held. Even though the bushwhackers who killed Gilmore were from another tribe, the frenzied soldiers called for the blood of Cornstalk and the other hostages. As the soldiers advanced through the door, Chief Cornstalk rose up and, standing erect, faced them. The sight of the bronzed six-foot chieftain bravely facing them caused the mob to pause, but only momentarily, before they opened fire, killing the Indians. The great Cornstalk went down, but not before eight musket balls tore into his flesh.

Red Hawk attempted to escape up the chimney

---

*Virginia originally included what is now West Virginia.

but was shot down. Ellinipsico was slain as he sat on a stool. The other Indian was slowly strangled to death. As Chief Cornstalk lay dying, he looked up at his crazed assassins, his eyes flashing with vengeance, and said, "I was the border man's friend. Many times have I saved him and his people from harm. I never warred with you, but only to protect our wigwams and our lands.

"I refused to join your paleface enemies with the Redcoats. I came to your fort as your friend, and you murdered me. You have murdered by my side, my young son."

The blood flowing from his wounds seemed to stop. He continued, "For this, may the curse of the Great Spirit rest upon this land. May it be blighted by nature. May it even be blighted in its hopes. May the strength of its peoples be paralyzed by the stain of our blood."

Then he lay down and died, his eyes still glaring at his killers.

The bodies of the other Indians, including Ellinipsico, were dumped unceremoniously into the Kanawha River. Chief Cornstalk was buried in a marked grave near the fort on Point Pleasant, overlooking the junction of the Ohio and Kanawha rivers.

In his book *Winning the West,* Theodore Roosevelt wrote, "Cornstalk died a grand death, by an act of cowardly treachery on the part of his American foes; it is one of the darkest stains on the checkered pages of frontier history."

The town of Point Pleasant was established in 1794. Through the years the chieftain's grave lay undisturbed. In 1840, his remains were removed to the grounds of the Mason County Court House where, in 1899, a monument was erected to his memory. At the dedication of the monument on October 13, Colonel C.E. Hogg commented that the chief "possessed the genius of Caesar," comparing his power with words to stir men's souls to heroic action with the ability of Patrick Henry.

In the late 1950's, when a new court house was built in Point Pleasant, the chief's remains, which consisted of three teeth and fifteen bones, or fragments of bones, were placed in an aluminum box and reinterred in a quiet corner of Point Pleasant's Tu-Endie-Wei* Park, beside the grave of a West Virginia frontiersman whom Cornstalk once fought and later tried to befriend. The D.A.R. erected a twelve-foot-tall monument to the chief.

There is another monument at Point Pleasant. It stands eighty-six feet tall and was dedicated August 22, 1909, a month late. Originally, it was to be dedicated on July 22, but at 11:30 p.m. on the night before the ceremony, a streak of lightning crashed down from a clear sky and struck the upper part of a derrick standing a hundred and five feet above the ground, badly damaging the machine. The crane was to be used the following day to set the monument in place— a monument in memory of the men who fell in the 1774 Battle of Point Pleasant, where Chief Cornstalk and the Indian Confederation were defeated.

The monument was finally dedicated and stood for years. Then, on July 4, 1921, another bolt of lightning shattered the stillness of Tu-Endie-Wei Park as it hit the monument erected in memory of the men who defeated Chief Cornstalk's warriors. The capstone and some granite blocks were knocked from the obelisk memorial. It was repaired and still stands today.

Could the lightning strikes have been acts of God, or were they the Shawnee chief's revenge—the Cornstalk Curse? Some people who live in the triangular area of western West Virginia, southwest Pennsylvania and southeast Ohio, say the curse is

---

*Tu-Endie-Wei is a Wyandot Indian term meaning "triangular point of land where two rivers meet."

only a legend—the result of imaginations that have grown with exaggeration down through the years. But there are also those who believe that the curse is real.

On April 21, 1930, three hundred and twenty persons perished in a fire at the State Penitentiary in Columbus, Ohio, eighty miles from Point Pleasant.

The worst American coal mine disaster, in number of lives lost, happened at Monongah, West Virginia, one hundred and ten miles from Point Pleasant, on December 6, 1907, when three hundred and ten miners died.

A hundred and fifty persons were killed on June 23, 1944, when a tornado ripped through the three-states triangular area at the junction of Ohio, Pennsylvania and West Virginia.

On November 14, 1970, a Southern Airways DC-9 crashed into a mountain near Huntington, West Virginia, forty miles from Point Pleasant, carrying seventy-five persons to their deaths, including the coaches and players of that city's Marshall University football team.

The Silver Memorial Bridge spans the Ohio River at Point Pleasant. It is called the Memorial Bridge in commemoration of the old Silver Bridge, which collapsed into the Ohio River in December 1967, hurling forty-six persons to their deaths.

The following August, a Piedmont Airlines plane crashed near Kanawha Airport killing thirty-five.

In February 1972, a wall of water from Buffalo Creek, a tributary of the Kanawha River, came roaring along an eighteen-mile canyon wiping out towns in its path and killing a hundred and twenty-five West Virginians.

In January 1978, a freight train derailed at Point Pleasant, dumping thousands of gallons of toxic chemicals, which seeped into the ground, contaminating the city's water supply wells, which had to be abandoned.

And then, on April 27, 1978, at the town of St.

Marys some fifty miles north of Point Pleasant, tragedy struck again. Fifty-one men, working on the Willow Island power plant construction site, were hurled to their deaths when a scaffold collapsed.

As far back as records of the area were kept, floods have periodically played havoc with riverfront towns on the Ohio and Kanawha rivers. Residents claim that the area is naturally prone to floods. If that is so, why do residents of the area keep erecting and rebuilding towns and buildings in the paths of sweeping flood waters?

And speaking of the Kanawha River, the oldest oil tanker serving with the U.S. Navy at the outbreak of World War II was the U.S.S. *Kanawha*. She was originally a coaling ship and was converted to a fleet oiler after World War I. On April 7, 1943, she was riding anchor at Tulagi in the Solomon Islands when the harbor was attacked by Japanese bombers. So confusing was the battle that gunners aboard the *Kanawha* shot down at least one of the U.S. planes.

After the raid, when the "all clear" was sounded, thirty-nine Japanese and seven American planes had been destroyed. The *Kanawha* was one of three U.S. ships sunk in the action. Did Chief Cornstalk's curse reach across the Pacific?

Jack Burdett, a Point Pleasant lawyer and historian, has researched the history of the area, including the Cornstalk Curse, for a number of years. He refers to the curse as "a compulsive bit of fascinating tradition, a unique part of the local nomenclature."

"I liken it to something not taken seriously. It's as commonplace as Murphy's law—something you can blame when things happen that shouldn't."

The historian recalled: "As a little child around here, whenever we were flooded by the Ohio River, which happened every other year, the grownups called it 'Cornstalk's Curse.'"

Although most of the folks living in the Cornstalk Curse area say the floods are no more than nature on the rampage, one wonders what makes nature go wild. What brings on the rains and snows that cause the floods? What caused Point Pleasant to be almost obliterated by floods in 1913 and 1937? It is a small town of about ten thousand, but why do so many strange things happen—like the barge explosion that killed six men just before Christmas in 1953? An entire city block was destroyed by a raging fire in the 1880's. In the last dozen years, fire destroyed or heavily damaged the Mason County Motor Car Company, the Sterling Hotel, the Quality Manufacturing Company, City Pharmacy, Murphy's Music Store, a Ben Franklin Store, Cohen's Drugstore, Christ Episcopal Church, the City Card Shop and Gene Ball's Restaurant.

Are the twelve-foot Cornstalk Monument and the aluminum casket containing the chieftain's bones all that remain of the great Shawnee leader? Or is there something else—something malefic—that endures? Could there be an imprecatory vestige of evil and death and impending disaster?—the origin of which derives from the dying words of Chief Cornstalk . . . "May the curse of the Great Spirit rest upon this land. May it be blighted by nature. May it even be blighted in its hopes. May the strength of its peoples be paralyzed by the stain of our blood."

These six words seem written in fire
on the walls of my cell,
"Nothing can be worse than this . . ."
                    "Machine-Gun" Kelly,
                    while on the Rock

". . . a private purgatory where carefully
chosen victims can slowly be driven mad."
                    The Birdman

13

On the Rock—Alcatraz

The Rock was the prison of prisons. Badmen, blood-letters and outlaws such as Al Capone, Alvin Karpis, "Machine-Gun" Kelly, Robert Franklin Stroud —"The Birdman"—and others found it the end of the line. For twenty-nine years, the fog-enshrouded Rock sealed off this country's most notorious criminals from the rest of the world. The grayness, damp winds, cold humidity and incessant foghorns made Alcatraz the loneliest of all America's penal bastions. From the time it became a federal prison in 1934 until it was closed down in 1963, her doors had clanged shut behind more than one thousand convicts. With few exceptions, they were the country's most hard-ened criminals and most skillful escape artists. It was because of them that the new prison was established to begin with.

Actually, Alcatraz was not a new prison per se. The island's original name was La Isla de Los Alcatraces, the Island of the Pelicans, when it was taken over in 1851 by the United States government.

In 1854, a lighthouse was established on Alcatraz to guide ships through the Golden Gate.

A few years later, an Army fort was erected on the island, and in 1859 Alcatraz saw its first prisoners—a contingent of court-martialed military convicts. During the Civil War years, the fort housed about a hundred Confederate Navy prisoners.

Indian chiefs and tribal leaders from Arizona and the Alaskan territories, who refused to give in to the demands of the white man during the 1870's and '80's, were incarcerated on the Rock.

With the coming of the Spanish-American War, the Rock became a bastille for Spanish prisoners brought over from the Philippines.

After the turn of the century, Alcatraz again became a disciplinary barracks for U.S. Army military incorrigibles.

The great earthquake that tore through San Francisco in 1906 left that city in shambles. A large fissure opened in the Rock, but the prison's buildings were left virtually unscathed. Prisoners from the heavily damaged San Francisco jail were temporarily housed on Alcatraz for safe-keeping until that city's prison was rebuilt.

Construction of new prison buildings on Alcatraz was started in 1906 and completed in 1909 by engineers and convicts of the U.S. Army. In 1911, the facility was officially named the United States Disciplinary Barracks . . . an Army prison.

In addition to Army prisoners taken during World War I, a number of seamen from impounded German vessels were interred on the Rock.

During the 1920's, Alcatraz gradually fell into disuse. Lighthouse keepers, some Army personnel and only a few of the most hardened Army disciplinary cases occupied the island.

When the Department of Justice decided in the early 1930's that the Rock would be ideally suitable as an escape-proof federal penitentiary, construction was begun on the new project. Practically the entire cell-block building was constructed atop the old Army fortress. Part of the Army prison was used, but the iron bars were replaced with bars of hardened tool steel. Gun towers were erected at vital locations around the island. Apartments for guards and their families were built on the old parade grounds; unmarried guards and support personnel would be housed in the same buildings that housed the Army guards. The lighthouse keeper's mansion—and it was a mansion—was taken over as the warden's residence, and another building was utilized for the lighthouse keepers.

Each convict train en route from the various federal prisons to Alcatraz usually had a celebrity aboard. The celebrity on the very first train in August 1934 was given the number eighty-five. As he was assigned his number, newspaper headlines across the nation were flashing his name: "CAPONE MOVED TO ALCATRAZ." But on the Rock, America's all-time number-one gangster, like his fellow prisoners, no longer had an identity other than his number.

Each cell in "America's first escape-proof prison" measured four feet by eight, had a single fold-up bunk, a toilet, a desk and chair and a sink. The "hole," as the solitary cells were referred to, were even smaller, and were bare except for a straw mattress which the guard removed each morning. There was no toilet—only a hole in the floor which was flushed from the outside. The prisoner sent to the "hole" was stripped naked and thrown onto the cell's cold concrete floor. When the bars clanged shut behind him, the guards slammed closed a heavy steel door just beyond the bars, engulfing the prisoner in total darkness. His diet of bread and water was supplemented by one solid meal every third day.

Alcatraz was not conceived as a facility for rehabilitation. It was a place of total punishment and minimum privilege. There were no trustees. It was strictly a punitive institution in which the inmates had but five rights: food, clothes, a private cell, a shower once a week and the right to see a doctor. In the "hole," all rights but the first were removed, and that remaining right barely sustained the convict's life, let alone his health.

When Warden Johnson and his cronies designed the new cell blocks, they overlooked one thing. Convicts thrown into the "hole" for anything but a minor infraction were usually severely beaten by guards who were as hardened as the convicts themselves. The screams from the men being beaten in one of the four "holes" situated on the lower tier of Block D echoed throughout that cell block as though the sounds were coming through a megaphone. The warden had designated all of Block D as a disciplinary unit. When the inmates of D heard a fellow convict being worked over in one of the "holes," they started a rumpus that was picked up by the prisoners in Blocks B and C (Block A was unused) that resounded across the island's twelve acres.

When they emerged from the "hole" after days, weeks or even months in the blackness, some of the men were totally senseless and had to be removed to a padded cell in the prison's hospital ward ... babbling idiots.

Others came out with pneumonia, or severely crippled by arthritis as a result of spending days lying on the cold cement floors without a stitch of clothing. Some men never emerged from the "hole"—alive.

In front of the unused Block A is a stairway that leads down to a heavy steel door. Behind that door are catacomb-like corridors framed by stone arches. Off the passageways are sealed-up gun ports from the days when Alcatraz was a fort. Fireplaces in several of the rooms off the corridors were never intended for warmth or comfort, but rather to heat cannonballs so they would start fires upon reaching their targets. Two of the other rooms were dungeons.

Prisoners placed in the dungeons were not only locked in, but also chained to the walls. Their screams could not be heard in the main prison. A bucket, emptied but once a week, served as a toilet. Every third day, the confinees got a full meal. In between, the prisoner in the dungeon received two cups of water and one slice of bread a day. He was chained to the damp wall in a standing-up position from six in the morning until six at night, after which he was given a blanket to rest on. He had no clothes whatsoever.

Three convict participants who survived Alcatraz' 1946 uprising were chained up in the dungeon. They were Clarence Carnes, Sam Shockley and Miran Thompson. Although the dungeon was used only on rare occasions, the dark cells of Block D, numbers eleven, twelve, thirteen and fourteen, or the "hole" as they were called by the inmates, were used regularly.

Capone was in the "hole" three times during his five-year stay on the Rock. The first years of the Rock were known as the "silent years," for no prisoners were allowed to speak to each other, sing or even whistle. Talking was forbidden in the cell block, the mess hall and the shower hall. The prisoners could talk for three minutes during the morning and afternoon recreation-yard periods, and on weekends for two hours.

Capone, who was quite arrogant when he arrived at the Rock, was unaware that the rule of silence also applied to him. Thus, twice he found himself in the "hole" for ten-day stretches for talking to other inmates. He also served nineteen days in the "hole" for attempting to bribe a guard for information on current events on the outside. Prisoners were not allowed newspapers, radios, magazines or anything else that could inform them of outside events. The only source of outside news came from newly arrived inmates. Although on all three occasions Capone emerged from the "hole" little the worse for his experience, the Rock would eventually break him.

Many of Alcatraz' prisoners ended up insane. In

1937 alone, fourteen of the prisoners went rampantly insane, and that number does not include those who slowly became "stir crazy." To Warden Johnson, mental illness was nothing more than an excuse to get out of work. It would be interesting to know what the warden thought when number 284, Rube Persfal, got hold of an ax, placed his left hand on a block of wood and, laughing maniacally, chopped off every finger on that hand. Then he placed his right hand on the block and pleaded with a guard to lop off that hand. Persfal was placed in the hospital, but not declared insane.

Joe Bowers slashed his own throat with his broken eyeglasses. He was given first aid and then thrown in the "hole." After his release, he broke away from his work area and scaled a chain-link fence, knowing the guards would shoot him. They did. He was dead when his body hit the rocks seventy-five feet below the fence.

Ed Wutke, an ex-seaman sentenced to twenty-five years for murder on the high seas, died after slicing through his jugular with a blade from a pencil sharpener. There were more attempts at suicide, and more men incurring mental breakdowns at Alcatraz, by percentage, than at any other federal prison.

Of all the attempted escapes from the Rock, only one prisoner is known to have made it ashore. John Paul Scott was recaptured while shivering among some rocks near the San Francisco side of the Golden Gate Bridge. Those who made it as far as the cold waters succumbed to the ever-churning eight-mile-per-hour currents that swirl seaward past the island. Although no bodies were ever recovered, the authorities assumed that the fugitives drowned, and marked the cases closed.

Attempts on Al Capone's life, the no-talking rule, ethnic slurs, beatings and a stabbing by other convicts, and prison routine began taking their toll on the ex-gangland chief. After several attempts on his life in the yard, he was excused from his yard privileges. Being quite adept with a banjo, he joined a four-man prison band. One of the other musicians, who played the drums, was "Machine-Gun" Kelly. Although gifts were not permitted, musical instruments were allowed. Al's wife, Mae, gave him a bejeweled banjo that cost over fifteen hundred dollars. After band practice, because of his fear of them, Capone was always back in his cell before the other convicts returned from the yard.

There were times when he refused to leave his cell to go to the mess hall to eat. He'd crouch down in a corner of his cell as though he were a cornered animal. On other occasions he would babble to himself in baby talk. As one fellow inmate said years later, "I remember every so often how he would repeatedly stay in his cell and make his bunk over and over."

Sometimes, Capone would strum on his banjo, singing "O Sole Mio" repeatedly. After five years on the Rock, the man who had Chicago eating out of the palm of his hand left Alcatraz on the verge of total insanity. He spent his last year in the hospital ward undergoing treatment for his condition, part of which was attributed to neurosyphilis—an advanced state of syphilis. Much of his time in the hospital was spent playing his banjo.

Capone's last day on the Rock was January 6, 1939. Thereafter, he was transferred to the New Federal Correctional Institution at Terminal Island near Los Angeles.

Jake "Greasy Thumb" Guzik, who was running the mob in Capone's absence, was asked by a reporter if Capone would take control again after his release. "Al," answered Guzik, "is nuttier than a fruitcake."

What was probably the most traumatic and violent happening at Alcatraz took place in 1946. It outshadowed by far the many murders and suicides that occurred on the island in previous years.

The Battle of Alcatraz started out as a well-planned and well-organized breakout from the "escape-proof" prison. In his book *Six Against the Rock*, Clark Howard provides a detailed hour-by-hour narrative of the battle.

In May 1946, six desperate inmates captured a gun cage, obtained prison keys and took over the cell house in less than an hour. The breakout attempt might have succeeded but for an ironic twist of fate. A guard, Bill Miller, didn't return one of the keys to the gun cage immediately after another guard finished with it, as required by prison regulations. It was an action for which Miller would have been reprimanded had the warden found out. But the only time Miller violated a security rule in his service as a prison guard happened exactly at the same time that the Rock's most desperate escape attempt took place. When the cons captured the gun cage, they found all of the keys except the one that would let them out of the cell building. That was the key Miller forgot to return to the Rock. Thus the breakout of the six desperate cons was thwarted before it began.

But the would-be escapees, Bernie Coy, Sam Shockley, Marvin Hubbard, Joseph Cretzer, Miran "Buddie" Thompson and Clarence Carnes, would not give up. Before the breakout attempt was over, nine guards were seized as hostages. Two of them were murdered in cold blood in cells 402 and 403, which were later changed to C-102 and C-104. Another guard would die later. Others were wounded.

Before the Battle of Alcatraz was over, two Navy destroyers, two Air Force planes, a company of Marines with mortars, a Coast Guard cutter, some Army officers, many policemen, a host of guards flown in from Leavenworth, and some from San Quentin were called in.

Three of the convicts—Coy, Hubbard and Cretzer—were slain in the utility corridor (a narrow hall between cell blocks, through which passed pipes, wiring and ventilation ducts). All three died from bullets and shrapnel with guns in their hands. An old Marine sergeant, who had been in the Corps almost as long as Robert Stroud had been in prison, cut a hole in the roof and dropped grenades down into the utility corridor where the three cons had taken refuge.

Thompson and Shockley were tried and sentenced to death. Carnes received life plus ninety-nine years. His life was spared because he helped some of the wounded guard hostages. The cell building was heavily damaged during the seige and took months to repair.

Every boatload of sightseers that arrives at Alcatraz is divided into groups, and a uniformed guide is assigned to each party. After a brief introduction to Alcatraz, the guide takes tourists on a long trek up the road to the top, with various stops en route. It is the same road up which Capone and the first contingent of convicts marched when they arrived at the Rock.

As a visitor, you'll eventually pass through the warden's office and the visiting room and enter the cell house. After leaving the deadlocked, double steel doors, you can look to the left and see at the east end of Block C just opposite the visiting room a steel door that looks as if it was once welded shut. Although the guides don't mention it, behind that door is the Block C utility corridor where Coy, Cretzer and Hubbard died in a hail of bullets and grenade shrapnel in 1946.

It was from behind this door that a night watchman heard strange, almost clanging-like sounds one night in 1976. Shining his flashlight down the corridor, he could see nothing but a maze of pipes and conduits. There were no sounds. When he closed the door, the noise began again. Again the door was opened, and still there was no one in the corridor. Believing neither in ghosts nor the supernatural, the watchman closed the door and continued on his way.

Whether the strange sounds coming from behind that door had anything to do with its having been once welded shut is not known.

Other night watchmen who've patrolled the cell house, after the last tourist boat has left for the day, have reported hearing sounds like footsteps of running men coming from the upper tiers, but subsequent investigations have showed nothing.

One Park Service employee mentioned that one rainy weekday morning, when there weren't enough sightseers to keep all of the guides busy, she was walking in front of Block A near the stairs leading down to the dungeons, when she heard a loud scream coming from behind the steel door at the bottom of those stairs. She fled without investigating. When I asked her why she didn't report the incident, she replied, "I didn't dare mention it because the day before, everyone was ridiculing another worker who reported hearing men's voices coming from the hospital ward, and when he checked the wards, they were empty."

"It's eerie out here," said one Park Ranger. "No way would I spend a night alone on the island."

Several of the guides and rangers expressed a strangeness about one of the "hole" cells—number 14-D. "There's a feeling of sudden intensity that comes with spending more than a few minutes around that cell. Maybe it's psychological from awareness of all the torment and suffering that went on in there," said another. "One day it got so bad that I turned and ran all the way down the hill to the office by the dock area. The next day," she continued, "I made myself go back up there and stand in front of fourteen-D because I knew if I didn't, it would have been impossible for me to work here on Alcatraz."

One guide who had remained silent at first now walked to the window. Staring out at the water he said, "That cell, fourteen-D, is always cold. It's even colder than the other three dark cells. Sometimes it gets warm out here—so hot that you have to take off your jacket. The temperature inside the cell house can be in the seventies. Yet, fourteen-D is still cold . . . so cold that you need a jacket if you spend any amount of time in it."

Another young woman added more to our information about 14-D: "Working in the area of Block D, especially near cell fourteen, really takes everything out of you emotionally. C'mon, let's go up there now and see how it affects you."

We trudged back up the hill for the second time that day, walked through the sally port and into the cell house. As we entered Block D, the last tour group of the day was passing through.

We waited until their guide had finished telling them about the "hole" and they had moved on. Then our escort took us into 14-D. Nancy walked through the doors first. Once inside the inner cell she held out her hands with her palms flattened. "My God, do I feel the emanations in here!"

I set my cameras down, entered the inner cell and held my hands out. I could feel an intense tingling sensation in my fingers. It was a feeling not unlike that of an arm or leg that has fallen asleep. I turned to the guide. "Come on in, and feel these vibes."

"No, I believe you. There's something in there. Try over in that corner," she said, pointing to a far corner of the room. "That's where the naked, shivering prisoners would huddle."

I moved over to the corner. Not only did the tingling in my hand intensify, but the temperature seemed much lower in about a two-foot-square area of the corner. Nancy moved next to me and said, "I've never felt so much energy before in one spot. I wish we could get a medium out here."

"A TV news team was going to stay all night on the island with a medium," commented our guide. "But at the last minute, the medium changed her mind and wouldn't come out."

What torture, what grief and what agony men must have endured in cell 14-D.

It was in 14-D that Rufe McCain was confined for three years and two months after an escape attempt in January 1939, during which the notorious "Doc" Barker was slain. When McCain emerged from the dark cell, he was virtually a madman. Eleven days later, McCain murdered a fellow convict, Hank Young, who had been a participant in the same escape attempt.

At his trial for the murder, McCain was found "not guilty" by the jury on the grounds that his years of confinement in the "hole" had deprived him of everything spiritual and human, and that his sense of morality was permanently destroyed. The general consensus of the jury was that it was the inhumanity of Alcatraz, and not McCain, that killed Young.

If, as many parapsychologists say, spirit entities, ghosts, apparitions and energy forces do haunt the places where they suffered the most traumatic experiences while they were alive, then Alcatraz must be loaded with them.

Chet Hendrix, an ex-cop who was badly shot up thwarting a warehouse robbery, now works nights as a private security guard on Alcatraz. On some nights he is the only living person on the Rock. We asked Mr. Hendrix if he ever had any strange or unusual experiences on his rounds. His reply was direct and to the point. "Sure, I've heard noises, such as men running, voices, whistling and doors closing. But I don't let them frighten me. You've got to remember that, with the wind blowing through all the broken windows in the cell house, and with all the seagulls and rats on the island, there are bound to be strange noises." He shifted his weight in his chair and continued, "But then again, there could be ghosts. Anything is possible."

A cold fog was moving in from the Pacific, almost enshrouding the Rock, as Nancy and I stood on the bridge deck of the boat taking us back to the mainland. The chill of the oncoming night was already penetrating our clothes. We were looking ahead at the lights of San Francisco when we heard a voice from behind us. It was a Park Service employee.

"Hi," he said. "You're the ones who're writing the book on ghosts, aren't you? I overheard some of your conversations back on the island. I myself heard something in the cell house early one morning. It was down in the shower room. A con killed his homosexual lover in there once—right in front of a guard. I guess it was a broken romance thing."

The boat changed course sending a sheet of spray past us. The young man shifted his hold on the stanchion he was hanging on to. "It's kind of strange what I heard. It was like banjo music. The room was empty, but I definitely heard banjo music coming from there. Maybe back in the days when it was a fort or an Army stockade, there was some guy here who played that instrument."

I looked back toward the Rock, now all but completely shrouded in fog, and thought of Al Capone during the most traumatic days of his life—when, rather than risk going out to the exercise yard with the other inmates, he sat in the shower room strumming on his banjo.

> So we beat on, boats against the current,
> borne back carelessly into the past.
>
> F. Scott Fitzgerald

14

The World's Largest
Haunted House—
Miami's Biltmore Hotel

Looking up at the towering three-hundred-foot structure on the north perimeter of the Biltmore Golf Course in Coral Gables, Florida, it is easy to reminisce of days that are gone forever. The old Miami Biltmore Hotel* goes back in time—more than fifty years.

It was an era of F. Scott Fitzgerald life-styles, and the Miami Biltmore was a southern showplace. Packards, Pierce Arrows, Stutzes and other great cars filled the hotel's shrub-lined drives, as their uniformed chauffeurs cooled in the shade of the royal palms. Multi-colored limousines delivered statesmen, financiers, captains of industry, sportsmen and the just plain rich up the curved ramp where a troupe of bellmen stood at attention, not unlike a squad of soldiers. Doormen, attired in uniforms that would be the envy of a Prussian general, clicked their heels as they opened handmade car doors. Strains of soft

---

*When the hotel was completed in 1925, Coral Gables was still part of the City of Miami.

music drifted from the afternoon dance taking place on the garden patio.

The main lobby, with its arches and columns, large enough to contain several two-story houses, was as brilliant and striking as any scene conjured out of the Arabian Nights. The drapes and furnishings in the lobby alone cost over a million dollars. The Biltmore had nothing but the best. Second best or compromise with cheapness was never tolerated.

In the main dining room, nearly half the size of a football field, the food went far beyond being merely delicious. The ceiling, thirty feet above the linen-covered tables, was bedecked with hand-painted murals.

The vast kitchens were manned by food specialists who acquired their finesse in such resorts as Ciro's, Cafe Marguery, Sherry's, Restaurant du Paris, the Savoy and other of the world's finest eateries. They were men who had pleased the palates of kings and queens, presidents, geniuses of finance and industry and both patrons and practitioners of the arts.

A tower of penthouses, called the Giralda Tower, reached up beyond the handmade Spanish-tiled roof topping the first ten floors. They were suites that ensconced such notables as President Coolidge, Gene Tunney, Paul Whiteman, Eddie Rickenbacker, Cornelius Vanderbilt, Jr., Jesse Lasky, Adolph Zukor, Bernard Baruch, the Duke and Duchess of Windsor, Ida Tarbell, Douglas Fairbanks and even Al Capone.

But today there is little left to recollect the luxurious dazzle that once prevailed—only vibrations and a feeling that the past may still be happening inside the vacant building.

The Great Depression of the 1930's had only a partial effect on the world's greatest hotel. However, with the United States' entry into World War II, the government took over the building as a training center for Marine officers.

When the war ended in 1945, the Veterans'

Administration purchased the Miami Biltmore Hotel for the purpose of using it as a hospital for men who returned from the war sick or wounded. With its five hundred rooms and well-designed layout, the building was perfect for a large hospital.

Not only did the huge structure serve to help the living, it was also a place for the dead. On the ground floor was a morgue that handled the many patients who died in the hospital. But there were other corpses at the hospital, too.

During the 1950's, a fire swept through part of the hospital ground floor. When firemen broke into the gutted section, they were greeted by the grisly scene of a room full of bodies charred beyond recognition. They didn't learn until later that the "fire victims" were part of the hospital's body collection.

There were several large tanks of formaldehyde that on occasion held as many as a hundred bodies at a time. The cadavers were being stored for medical-school students at the University of Miami. Thus, the Coral Gables veterans hospital housed the ill, the dying and the dead.

In 1965, a new Veterans' Administration hospital was completed at a modern hospital complex in Miami, and the old Coral Gables structure was vacated. Today, aside from being a towering landmark reminiscent of a more glorious era, the old Biltmore serves no purpose. The building was deeded over to Coral Gables in the early 1970's.

Inside the hotel, the once majestic lobby is now forlorn and empty. The huge chandeliers draped in cobwebs no longer glitter in the dim light. The stone gargoyles guarding the tiled staircases are covered with dust. The main desk, where Who's Who in American society once signed the guest registration book, is littered with debris. Some of the marble top is missing—probably pilfered. Hand-carved African mahogany panels are camouflaged under layers of green G.I. paint.

The Biltmore's elevator, unlike others, indicated a

thirteenth floor. On the thirteenth was the Royal Penthouse Suite, which included the fourteenth floor. These were two floors of pomp and artistry that outshined even the elegant lobby. The fourteenth floor was actually a mezzanine of rooms that surrounded the arched and columned thirteenth. One could look down from the balcony at the ballroom-like thirteenth-floor living room and see the largest stone fireplace ever built so high up in a building. The thirteenth floor didn't always serve as a lodging for the elite, however. It also served a more sinister purpose. For the thirteenth-floor Royal Penthouse Suite was once the setting for terror and death.

Up and down New York's "Great White Way" in the 1920's, the initials "A.R." meant Mr. Big. A.R. was a millionaire gambler who could fix anything: court cases, bets, a night in bed with a Broadway actress, murder, and even a sporting event such as the 1919 World Series, in which eight players for the Chicago White Sox received seventy thousand dollars in bribes. Mr. Big was in reality the uncrowned king of the underworld—Arnold Rothstein.

Almost every night, Mr. Big would have his chauffeur-driven Packard parked at the curbside near Forty-ninth Street and Broadway. There he'd get out and walk the seven blocks to Times Square and back. During his walk, A.R. never hesitated to place a bet with the many sharpies who courted his trade. It was not unusual for him to carry more than two hundred thousand dollars on his person, and to bet with crisp new thousand-dollar bills.

Back in those days, that section of Broadway wasn't polluted with pimps, drug pushers, prostitutes and cheap X-rated movie houses as it is today. Then, Times Square and the adjacent area was the place where anybody who was anybody in show business headed. It was tourism's greatest drawing card.

Still, Rothstein was always flanked by a cordon of

bodyguards. These men were rough-and-tough individuals who would kill an adversary without batting an eyelash. They were highly paid and their manner of dress showed it. Mr. Big's number-one bodyguard was Thomas Walsh, sometimes called "Whitey," and sometimes called "Fatty."

"Fatty" Walsh, balding and fortyish, had been in the rackets since his early youth. Wherever Rothstein went, Walsh went, too.

Then, one day in October 1928, Fatty decided that he wanted to go out on his own. He and A.R. parted on good terms and remained friends. They were such good friends that a month later on November 4, when Rothstein was mortally wounded at the Park Central Hotel after welching on a bet, Walsh was at his bedside in the Polyclinic Hospital when he died.

Fatty Walsh was questioned by police about who might have killed his ex-boss, but he said nothing.

Several weeks later, the New York police again sought to question Walsh, but this time it was about his possible knowledge of a big New York City jewel heist. Thinking that Florida's sunshine might offer a healthier climate, Fatty headed south before the police were able to question him.

Accompanying Walsh was a close friend and fellow underworld character, thirty-year-old Arthur Clark. In appearance, the two men presented a stark contrast. Walsh was six feet tall and on the heavy side. Clark was a head shorter, skinny, dark complected and weasel-faced.

When the two men arrived in Miami, they rented an apartment on Ferdinand Street in Coral Gables. Their only run-ins with the law in Florida concerned complaints of noisy parties in their apartment. At one of his parties, Walsh met a former acquaintance, Edward Wilson, a wealthy New York City and Chicago gambler.

Wilson had leased the Royal Penthouse Suite on the thirteenth and fourteenth floors of the Biltmore Hotel. With the knowledge of the hotel's operators, and probably most law-enforcement agencies, Wilson ran a combination gambling casino and plush speakeasy in the Biltmore's tower. Just as the working class had their back-room speakeasys at which to buy liquor during the Prohibition era, the well-to-do of Miami and Coral Gables had their Biltmore Tower.

Somehow, either by choice or necessity, Wilson took Fatty Walsh in as a partner in his operation. Apparently, Fatty gave his new business associate a break on liquor prices, for he owned the Federal Liquor Company in Havana, Cuba, which was a major supplier to South Florida bootleggers. Fatty's booze supply house was financed by loans obtained from New York underworld syndicates.

The casino partnership was rocky, encouraging little love between Fatty and Wilson. Wilson thought he'd given Fatty too much of the partnership, and Walsh felt he didn't get enough. One night, things came to a head between the two men.

Shortly after midnight on Thursday morning, March 7, 1929, over a hundred formally clad people were at the bar or gaming tables thirteen and fourteen floors up in the Biltmore's Giralda Tower. Black ties, tuxedos, derby hats, flowing gowns and mink stoles dominated the scene. Only the finest imported (smuggled) liquor was being served. Diamond-clad fingers reached for cards or tossed dice. A trio of musicians in the balcony were competing with the sounds of clacking dice, spinning roulette wheels and murmuring voices as they played "Alexander's Ragtime Band."

Two men were arguing in a card room off the main casino hall. They were tall and hefty Fatty Walsh, and gray-haired five-foot-four, hundred and sixty pounder Ed Wilson. Because of the other noises, no one else could tell what the subject of their dispute was, except that it had something to do with money. The two men swore at each other, then Wilson walked away and sat down on a divan where he watched several men at the blackjack table. Fatty began pacing back and forth on the other side of the room.

At the same time the band finished "Alexander's Ragtime Band," Fatty sat down on a straight-backed chair next to the card table with his back to Wilson.

An instant later, Wilson jumped up from the divan and drew a .38-caliber revolver loaded with copper-jacketed bullets. As he backed toward the door leading to the main room, a pall of silence fell over the fifteen or so people in the small room.

As Fatty started to turn around, a shot was fired from Wilson's pistol, passing through his right side before ricocheting off the tabletop. Fatty started to fall and Wilson fired another shot that hit Walsh before he struck the floor.

As Fatty Walsh lay face down on the floor, his head under the gaming table, the chair he'd been sitting on toppled across his legs. His friend Art Clark ran across the room and knelt at his friend's side. Wilson fired another shot. The bullet hit Clark, passing through his left arm and striking a rib that deflected the bullet out through his chest.

Still holding his gun, Wilson backed out of the door, turned around and ran across the large room, bumping into some of the people standing at one of the roulette tables in the process. Women screamed and men yelled, but no one made an effort to stop the killer, who was charging toward the entry hall.

As Wilson ran into the hall and headed for the upstairs, the crowd panicked, for no one wanted to get involved in the investigation that was sure to ensue. During the stampede one woman, the wife of a New York City subway official, was thrown against the sharp metal edge of a table, causing lacerations to her face and right arm. Wilson himself was last seen dashing across the downstairs lobby and out toward the parking lot.

A Rookie patrolman had just reported for duty when

Sergeant Brasher told him, "Get the car ready. There's been a shooting at the Biltmore."

The plain black Model-T Ford touring car that the two policemen arrived in looked out of place among the elite motor cars parked in the Biltmore's driveway. The two officers entered the lobby and walked to the elevators.

Both elevators were on upper floors. The two policemen waited. The elevators moved but a floor or two at a time, never getting closer to the lobby than the fourth floor. After ten minutes, Sergeant Brasher turned to his young colleague and said, "C'mon, let's take the stairs. Someone's playin' games with the elevators."

The officers found the door to the stairwell locked. Brasher went to the front desk and demanded to know what was going on. "You got two minutes to open that stairwell door or I'm going to have the Fire Department come and break it in!"

Just as the sergeant was about to call the Fire Department, the Rookie came over to him. "Both elevators have come down," he said.

When the two policemen entered the Royal Penthouse Suite, they found the rooms barren of all furnishings. Even the rugs had been removed. In a little room off the main room was a dead body lying on the floor. It was covered with a white linen sheet. Standing next to the corpse was a man with his arm and chest covered with bloodstained bandages. The sergeant bent over and pulled the sheet halfway down.

Fatty Walsh, the man who once walked proudly under the glittering lights of Broadway with Mr. Big, lay lifeless—his eyes closed forever.

While being led to an ambulance, Clark sobbed, "He was shot down like a dog. He never had a chance."

Obviously, the elevators had been intentionally delayed in order to remove the liquor bar and gambling paraphernalia from the murder scene.

When the scene was reconstructed for a reenactment of the crime, none of the gambling devices or original gaming tables were returned to the rooms.

Six individuals were held and questioned as material witnesses. One was a man named M.D. Simpson.

Demaris Dove, an eighteen-year-old nightclub hostess who had witnessed the shooting of Mr. Big, was also present at Fatty's demise. After the shooting, she had fled screaming upstairs to a room at the southeast corner of the fourteenth floor. New York police questioned her for ten hours before releasing her.

For several weeks, law-enforcement agencies sought Wilson, but he was nowhere to be found. Almost a month later, word leaked out through the grapevine that on the night after the murder of Fatty Walsh, Ed Wilson was seen at the Miami airport being placed aboard a Havana-bound Ford tri-motor plane by agents of the Dade County District Attorney's Office.* Other rumors suggested that certain law-enforcement agencies were receiving 10 percent of the profits from the gambling operation at the Miami Biltmore.

It is not known what happened to Clark after he left the hospital; however, he was being sought by both the New York City and Philadelphia Police Departments for running confidence games.

As for Wilson, he was unheard of until many years later. In 1946, the chief of the Coral Gables police received a call from the Federal Bureau of Investigation in Los Angeles. They were checking on a man named Wilson. He apparently was connected in some way with Paramount Pictures. He had confessed to the F.B.I. that he was the same Wilson connected with the slaying of Thomas "Fatty" Walsh. The F.B.I. asked for a report of the incident. The Chief told him that there was no report. "How can you be

---

*Since changed to the State Attorney's Office.

so sure when you haven't looked?" the F.B.I. man questioned.

"Because," answered the chief, "I was there and at that time no report was required. Things have changed since then, but the only records that existed then were in our heads."

It has been a half century since Thomas "Fatty" Walsh met his Maker. But did he meet his Maker? Does his spirit still roam? Is Fatty one of the numerous entities that still haunt the old Miami Biltmore Hotel–Veterans' Administration hospital in Coral Gables, Florida?

Nancy Osborn and myself, along with four members of the Arthur Ford Academy and one from the Spiritual Frontiers Society, visited the Miami Biltmore Hotel in May 1978. Our companions were Patricia Hayes, Jan Clema, Ann Phillips, Jean Barr and J.R. Worden. All are qualified mediums or parapsychologists. Each had proven his or her ability to communicate with the spirit world on numerous occasions in the past. Patricia Hayes and J.R. Worden did psychical research for John Fuller's book, *Flight 401.* None of the five was informed as to where they were being taken.

As we entered the structure's ground floor, I led the group through the dimly lit debris-strewn lower lobby directly to the rooms where the morgue had once been. I was sure that they would pick up something, for there had to have been several thousand or more autopsies done there during the years when the Veterans' Administration had the building.

I watched from the hallway as the group entered the autopsy room, wondering if they would sense something in these rooms where so many dead bodies had been. But there was no reaction. It was then explained to me that ghosts and other such entities choose to hang around where something happened during their lifetime rather than after their death.

I thought of several city workers who told me of unusual noises which were heard in the building. I pondered on what one city official said, that no city employees had been allowed unarmed in the structure after dark or at any time without a two-way radio. I thought of the private security guard who patrols the grounds at night, but who is not allowed anywhere in the old hotel except for several rooms on the ground floor. Then I remembered what the official said about the maintenance crew that went into the morgue to clean up, then fled the building and refused to go back in.

Back in the lower lobby, we stood in front of the elevator. "Something happened here," called out Hayes. "I don't know what, but right here on this spot something happened. I have a feeling that we should go upstairs."

One floor up, in the main lobby, all five psychics again picked up vibes as we passed the elevators. "Something happened in this building," said Worden, "and the elevators were somehow involved."

Phillips added, "There was a lot of commotion here."

Barr placed her hand on the elevator button. "Whatever they were excited about didn't happen here. It took place upstairs."

Hayes said, "Let's work our way up, floor by floor. We'll stop at each landing and see if we can pick up anything."

We started up the stairs. The steps were littered with beer cans, fallen plaster, old papers and other debris. Between the time that the United States government owned the building and when it was turned over to the City of Coral Gables, a number of hippies and derelicts inhabited the structure.

Between the ninth and tenth floors, the group stopped. Hayes' eyes scanned the stairwell. "We're being followed," she said. "We're not alone. There are others on these stairs." I looked down to where we had been, but I couldn't see anything.

"There are four men following us," said Worden. "They've been with us since we left the lobby." I looked around again and saw nothing. We resumed our climb.

It wasn't until we reached the thirteenth floor that some unseen force or energy appeared to act abruptly on the entire group. I, myself, felt nothing. I'm a "show me, and I'll believe you" type of individual—so I was very busy looking around for visual apparitions.

There was no signal or communication among the others. It was just a simultaneous reaction. "There's something here on this floor," said Worden.

Ann Phillips stood mutely looking up the stairwell toward the fourteenth floor. Without saying a word, Barr opened the door leading from the stairwell into the thirteenth-floor Royal Penthouse Suite. As she left the stairwell, it was as though she was in some kind of a trance. The others followed. I looked at Nancy. I could tell that something was affecting her, too. It was as though she was oblivious to me. I was the last one into the suite. It was like a large amphitheater—a huge room with a huge fireplace surrounded by a balcony and mezzanine that was really the fourteenth floor.

Each of the mediums seemed to be wandering off in a different direction. As they checked out the rooms, I watched silently. "It's not here," said Hayes. "It's up there on that balcony." The group had all been drawn toward the stairs. I followed them up.

At the top, I expected them to work around the balcony. But, instead, they silently entered a room at the southeast corner of the mezzanine without even checking the balcony. The group talked among themselves.

"There's someone in here."

"It's an entity that wants to talk to us."

"Something happened in this suite and this particular room was involved."

They were talking so fast, I couldn't tell who was

saying what. "Is it the four that were following us up the stairs?" I asked.

"No, they left us when we entered this suite," answered Phillips. "They don't like this suite."

Nancy began to unfold a blanket she was carrying. Hayes grabbed one end of it, and they spread it out on the floor. The group sat down in a circle on the blanket and joined hands. The room became quiet. As I was leaning over, setting up the tape recorders in the center of the circle, Hayes said, "Oh, can I feel the energy!"

An instant later, for no apparent reason, one of the venetian blinds tore loose from the wall and crashed to the floor. Both Nancy and I jumped. The others were deep in thought and oblivious to the falling blinds. Hayes said, "The energy is going around the circle to the right. As soon as you feel it in both hands, say 'O.K.' "

"Lighter and lighter, clearer and clearer. We are gathered here for the purpose of a séance. We ask if there are any entities around the circle and will they help us?"

The mediums let go of each others' hands and turned their palms up. All had their eyes closed. One of the group said, "There was lots of partying and a lot of drinking here. I'm not feeling an old person."

Hayes: "I get a young woman, maybe thirty."

Clema: "She's looking for a child, a baby."

Worden: "It's a boy. He saw her die."

Phillips: "It wasn't in this room. But it wasn't far away, either."

Barr: "She was murdered and now she seeks her child."

Phillips: "First, I'm getting the persons are here because they can't leave. They're earthbound. They are bound here because of some unfinished business."

Worden: "Somehow, the true story never has been brought out."

Hayes: "I see a story in a newspaper, though. I see a column in the newspaper."

Worden: "Boy, did I get a pain in my neck then. Whew!"

Someone else: "This was the room they felt best in. What happened could be below us."

Phillips: "He's making me nervous."

Osborn: "Who's making you nervous?"

Phillips: "The little old man with a cane."

Hayes: "He just keeps walking in circles around us."

Worden: "He won't participate with us."

Hayes: "He's curious. He only wants to observe, but his tapping cane is bugging us!"

There seemed to be a consensus that whatever happened occurred by the fireplace down on the thirteenth floor. Someone said, "A girl or a very young woman, she saw it and ran upstairs to this corner room. She wasn't involved."

Someone asked, "How did she die?"

Clema: "By my own hand. By my own hand. She was an unstable person."

Phillips: "She leaped or jumped." She pointed to the back of her neck. "This part of her is hurting."

Clema: "It was many years later. And I don't think it was here in this building."

Someone else: "Whatever happened here, happened at night. There are people running around."

Hayes: "There's something we're missing. It's not all together."

Winer: "What happened by the fireplace?"

Barr: "I feel there was an argument by the fireplace . . . a serious argument—two men."

Worden: "I'm getting an overall picture of more violence than what we've been talking about. There was much more violence. They are trying to tell us something."

Hayes: "One person is trying to do something with his hands. This person holds back one hand. All right, let's focus in there. All right, c'mon!"

Barr: "They're arguing about security or something."

Winer: "Did someone depart this earthly world from here, or down by the fireplace in the drawing room?"

Hayes: "Yes, definitely. It might be two people."

Winer: "Violently?"

Hayes: "Yes, one person violently. Unnatural death is violent, and one was very violent. One died by a sharp instrument. There's too much pain for it to be dull, a knife or . . ."

Worden: "There is something written that is supposed to be very important, too. It was written by one of the parties concerned. It was written in a heavy hand."

Phillips: "I'm seeing a scene which appears to be in the lobby. There are frightened people and something has happened here. In the lobby where we first walked in there's commotion."

Worden: "This has a feeling of a type of opera. If we could just analyze it somewhere along the line."

Hayes: "I pick up something happening downstairs."

Phillips: "It seems near the front entrance, not by the desk, but it's like they came down—I see a man, a pasty-faced fellow. He was one of those arguing. I see him running across a room and down the stairs all the way to the lobby. He's obviously upset."

Hayes: "There appears to be a lot of blood."

Winer: "The murder weapon, what was the murder weapon?"

Hayes: "Well, it was fast. It isn't a hammer— nothing dull. A bullet is sharp. So is a knife. It was something that went right in. This didn't take place in our time."

Barr: "It's like something happened to him, and they didn't know what to do with him. I don't feel that the police were called."

Hayes: "Well, anyway, there was sure a lot of commotion. I'm getting a lot of commotion, too, from outside sources. Something came in from outside."

Winer: "Were the police here?"

Clema: "I think the police were here on a superficial level; what really happened was never shown or told. But I do think the police were brought in."

Worden: "O.K.! I've had someone come in, but I can't get a good communication with him. It's an old man, wheelchair, snow-white hair, a full head of hair and black-framed glasses. He seems to know something but he won't say what it is. He's also an observer here. It seems he doesn't fit in with this, but he knows all about it. He's been into the hospital part of this thing."

Hayes: "The number sixty-seven keeps coming back. There's still something very important that's missing. We need a first name to work on and nothing more."

Osborn: "Try Fats. It's a nickname."

Hayes: "Come on, Fats. The vibration just won't come. Come on in, Fats. We want to talk to you. We want someone who can tell us something clear. Come on, you had a good mind. Just think what you want us to hear. Just think it."

Clema: "I'm getting energy on the back of my neck, very prickly. There's gambling or something."

Hayes: "Like someone said earlier, there's something secretive going on here. Yes, there is. I see numbers in front of me now. Come in, Fats, come on in. What have you got for us. He's a religious man in his own stupid way."

Phillips: "I see numbers that I associate with gambling. What's numbers got to do with it?"

Hayes: "O.K. Let's concentrate on what happened."

Phillips: "I don't feel anyone in close."

Hayes: "I feel there was some sort of a warning about something. Yes, I feel there was someone being told something, and a lot of fast action right after that, and then I saw some small slips of paper being secretly handed back and forth. There was a message passed, and the action started after that, but there was no time to do anything about it. There was a warning through someone."

Clema: "I feel people coming from outside of the building as part of the warning, or perhaps they're the people warned about."

Hayes: "I know there was one murder, but were two people killed at the same time? I think maybe . . ."

Barr: "I get the name Dominic."

Hayes: "Fats was a very highly motivated person. He had to have a reason for everything he did."

Worden: "I have him always holding on to things. Seems he didn't want to let go of anything."

Hayes: "I'm not so sure he's a trustworthy person."

Worden: "The observer in the wheelchair is telling me there's a story to be told here, and it isn't being told."

Winer: "Tell him if he comes through, we'll give him some information."

Clema: "This man has done more dealing and double-dealing."

Winer: "If he agrees, we'll tell him first."

Hayes: "Fats, do you want to know? I'm picking up his curiosity. There was more energy coming in when you said that. I think he—I was going to say, he's trying to tell us something about a man who looks like a 'weasel.' "

Clema: "I just felt a little person beside him, when you said that, and he looks just like a little weasel. This little guy looks slick to me. He dresses very well and is short. He's swarthy and darker-complexioned than the other guy. Fat's question is, 'Was it the little weasel?' "

Worden: "Fats is a very manipulative personality. He was one to pull strings."

Hayes (laughs): "You got him curious."

Clema: "First of all, I felt gurgling caused by blood in the throat and chest."

Winer: "Yes, but what caused the choking by blood in the throat and chest? What caused it?"

Clema: "I just get the gurgling of blood in my throat."

Hayes: "I couldn't say it was a knife, but someone was close physically when they killed him."

Winer: "Tell us what the murder weapon was, Fats. We know what happened to the culprit. But you're going to have to come through to us. You were a big wheeler-and-dealer, but we are probably the last ones on this earth who will communicate with you. If you don't try to come through soon, we're going to try to contact one of the other spirits who're hanging around here. Now, come on, Fats. You can go on eternally wondering what happened to that man who killed you. It's up to you. You have nothing to lose by talking and everything to gain."

Hayes (to Winer): "He likes you." (She laughs aloud.)

Clema: "It's a gun, a handgun."

Hayes: "There are several around; this crowd carries guns."

Barr: "I see a gun that is rounded at the handle."

Winer: "What about the gun?"

Barr: "I don't know what you call it, but two shots were fired."

Hayes: "There was a lot of mess."

Winer: "O.K., if it was a gun, can you tell how many times he was shot?"

Hayes: "It was sure more than once! There were probably two shots fired, but they were so close together it sounded like one. You've got to realize that Fats might not know the answer to the question you're asking. It depends on how quickly he died and which bullet killed him. The killer wanted to make sure Fats was dead. He wanted the job done."

Phillips: "I feel something in the chest, close to the heart."

Winer: "We'll give you part of the answer now, Fats. We'll keep our bargain with you. The culprit is still alive, and he was never punished for the crime. The statute of limitations ran out. He turned up in California. He got off scot-free, and he's still alive today after all these years!"

Phillips: "For some reason, Fats is saying, 'I hope he lives another hundred years.' The killer is suffering."

Barr: "Yes, he's suffering. He's not a well man."

Osborn: "Has Fats made any advancement spiritually since his death? Has he become a better person?"

Hayes: "No, he's pretty much the same as he was when he lived in this world."

Winer: "Does Fats want to leave the world of spirit he's in now, and make progress in another dimension?"

Clema: "Do you mean, does he want to leave the world he's in now? No, he's earthbound. He likes what he's doing now. He's manipulating through other people."

Phillips: "He's still doing what he loves to do. He was involved in a lot of shady deals."

Hayes: "In fact, I don't know what he had to do with jewels; maybe he just liked jewelry. But I feel he is still connected with jewelry. He could be in New York. He's still wheeling and dealing—very much in motion and in the action . . . When he first came in and looked around, it was you [looking at Winer] that caught his interest, or he wouldn't have talked to any of us."

Winer: "Is he communicating with anyone in our world?"

Hayes: "He's working through people in our world —people who are unaware that he's manipulating them."

Winer (after several minutes of silence by the group): "Can we get anything more from him, or is he finished?"

Worden: "I haven't been able to hold anything for the last five minutes."

After the séance, we went back down to the thirteenth floor, where we gathered around the fireplace. Clema walked over to a window facing south. Putting both hands on the glass she said, "Someone jumped from this window."

"Was it during the murder?" I asked.

The tall brunette kept looking out over the golf course thirteen floors below. "No, it happened many years later. Maybe in the late 1930's."

"We're not by ourselves in here," muttered Hayes. "There are many entities in this room. A presence of death is over to the left of the fireplace."

"Maybe someone died in that room there," commented Osborn.

"I see a man with a surgical mask and hat, wide, deep-set eyes, large build, large shoulders, muscular, athletic, vain, and he has a lot of self-confidence—almost to the point of conceit."

"He's a lover. Might be a Scorpio," said someone else.

As I was kneeling to change the cassette in the tape recorder, I heard another voice describe a couple with an Afghan hound. "He's dapper, with slick black hair, slight build, about six feet six or seven inches tall. He's got a full mustache and carries an ebony cane with a gold knob. Made his money quickly. His wife's a plain-Jane type. He brags. Received the name Simpson."

The group went on for several minutes describing various entities that were around us. I asked, "How many spirits are there in this building? Could there be a hundred?"

Hayes replied, "From all of the force and activity going on in here, there are probably hundreds of them."

As we reached the ground floor and passed in front of the elevator again, all five of the mediums exhibited some concern. Hayes turned and said, "Yes, something sure went on right here when Fats was killed."

While we were standing by our cars before going

our separate ways, I again asked Patricia Hayes how many ghosts or entities she felt really inhabited the old Biltmore Hotel. She slid behind the wheel of her Volkswagen and said, "Well, Dick, I can't really say for sure. Some come and go. They don't necessarily hang around a place just because they died there. More often they'll haunt a locale where something significant happened to them while they were alive. But that's not to say they don't ever return to the place of their death. You saw that today. Fats didn't come here as a guest. He had some tie-in with the hotel or its operation."

Again, I asked her, "Pat, how many spirits, ghosts or entities would you estimate to be dwelling in this building?"

She started the engine of her little car, looked up at me and said, "From the quantity revealed today during the short time we were in the building, there could be a thousand. Who can say for sure? We are dealing with a different concept of time and space here. Our reality contains only one dimension, but it's a multi-dimensional universe." She shifted the car into gear and drove off.

That evening I received a telephone call from Nancy. "Hey, I got all prepared to start transcribing the séance tapes, and, well, we've got a problem."

"Don't tell me they didn't record," I interrupted.

"No," she replied. "It's not quite that bad, but we've got a terrible ticking noise all the way through the séance. I'll bring it over and you can listen for yourself."

When she got to my house, she flicked on the tape recorder about a third of the way into the cassette. She was right. There was a steady ticking sound, like a metronome that had gone haywire. "Run it back to the beginning," I said.

"Testing one, two, three" were the first words on the tape. There was no ticking noise on that part.

When the recorder was turned on at the start of

the séance, there also was no ticking. We listened to the recording of the session, wondering what happened to the ticking sound. Then we heard the sound of the ticking. It was very faint at first but got louder. It came on just when the tape got to the part where Patricia Hayes asked any entities around the circle to help us. The tapping continued through the ceremony as we listened. At times it was so loud that listening to the mediums' words became difficult.

When the playback came to the part where Phillips said, "He's making me nervous," and Osborn asked, "Who's making you nervous?" my skeptical disbelief began to diminish. For then they started talking about the little man whose tapping cane annoyed them. The sound was just like the noise of a tapping cane—almost like a blind man feeling his way. It lasted to the end of the cassette. The séance had finished while I was reversing the cartridge.

I turned the cassette over and ran some recording tests. There was no sound of tapping on the new recording. Then, I placed the cassette in another recorder and replayed the séance tape. The tapping was still there. I then rewound the cassette to the beginning and transferred the entire side with the sitting, including the test at the beginning of the tape, onto a seven-inch reel-to-reel tape machine. Still the tapping sound was on the tape from where the mediums first picked up the energy to the end of the cartridge.

Did we pick up the sound of a spiritual entity's tapping cane during the séance? I can think of no other thing that could cause such a noise, especially at the point where it began on the tape. Had it been all the way through, even on the test part at the beginning, then it could be attributed to a mechanical malfunction. The chances of the tape itself being defective are so remote that they are not even worth considering. For look at the odds of a tapping noise caused by a defective tape starting just as the séance was getting underway.

Another thought came to mind. Maybe one of the participants had a noise-creating device secreted on his or her person. But that, too, is impossible, for we had a second tape recorder, one that was even more sensitive than the first, turned on during the séance. It has a good identical track of the séance, but there are no sounds whatsoever of the tapping noise.

The single-track cassette has not been tampered with, and to have added the tapping noise would erase the original track on the tape. To have put the tapping on first would also not have worked, for that sound would have been erased when the séance was recorded over it.

That leaves only one other possibility. The tapping could actually have originated from the cane of the little old man's ghost as he observed the séance. Then, of course, how did the tape recorder pick up a sound inaudible to my ear? Nancy's reply to this question was, "The same way that ghosts who are invisible to a photographer's eyes show up later in a picture taken by that cameraman."

After concluding that there appears to be no earthly explanation for the tapping sounds on the tape recording of the séance, Nancy and I began our research into microfilms, old newspapers, archives and any other source of information on the old Miami Biltmore Hotel and the Coral Gables veterans' hospital. Of several interviews, one proved most interesting.

William Guerrant Kimbrough retired as chief of the Coral Gables Police Department on December 31, 1977, after serving almost fifty years with that department. A plaque in the lobby of the Coral Gables Police Department commemorates his years of service. Chief Kimbrough joined the Coral Gables police force in late 1928 as a replacement for an officer killed on duty on Christmas Day of that year.

Kimbrough was twenty years old when he strapped on his gun. He was assigned to work with Sergeant Floyd Brasher, who was to train him on the job.

It was nearly fifty years later that Nancy and I visited Bill Kimbrough at his Coral Gables home. He cordially invited us in to his living room, where we explained that we were researching some incidents that occurred at the old Biltmore Hotel. He looked at us in a peculiar way when we explained that we had held a séance in the old building. However, his cynical look gradually turned to surprise as he read Nancy's transcript of the mediumistic session. He was especially astonished at the part about something having happened in front of the elevators that was related to the shooting. "It was," he said, "something no one, not even the papers, knew about. In fact," he continued, "there are many things in the transcript of the séance that were never brought out before."

Our research in the archives of the Miami Public Library, the microfilms of the *Miami News* and other local papers verified enough of our findings to show that what came out in the séance was better than 90 percent right.

Let's weigh the facts. Remember, the five mediums who were taken into the old building had no idea as to where they were going until an hour or two before. That hardly gave them time to research the building's history.

They, the mediums, picked the right floor where the murder took place. After some difficulty, they were able to determine that it was bullets and not a knife or other sharp instrument that did the killing. Although they picked up two shooting murders on that floor, there were two men shot—one was killed, one was wounded. That's still pretty close.

The confusion at the elevator was not mentioned

in any newspaper. Only Chief Kimbrough verified that it happened, and that it was directly related to the murder.

They picked up the near panic that took place in the casino after the shooting. And they also brought out the fact that two men argued before the shooting. Likewise, they were correct in determining that the events occurred at night.

According to our research, many of the details about the murder and the casino operation were covered up by high-up law-agency officials. That was mentioned during the séance when Clema talked about what really happened not having been shown or told to the press. And as to gambling having taken place in the suite, all of the mediums picked up on that. Concerning the pieces of paper having been passed back and forth, that could well have been the concealing of the casino receipts.

Hayes told of Fatty's spirit mentioning something about a small man who looked like a weasel. Studying photographs of Arthur Clark, it is obvious that he was a small weasel-faced man. Is Fatty looking for his old friend? It could be that Clark could still be alive and has yet to enter the spirit world. If he were alive he'd be close to eighty.

It was mentioned in the séance that Fatty was somehow connected with jewelry. The New York City Police Department was seeking to question him about a big jewel heist in that city.

Nancy and I were previously told that Fatty was from Chicago. But actually, as brought out accurately in the séance, he was from New York.

During the séance, someone said the name "Simpson" was received. One of the material witnesses held for questioning was named M.D. Simpson.

Clema said during the séance that someone jumped from a window, that it happened many years after the murder, maybe in the late 1930's. We could find no record of anyone having jumped from the thirteenth or fourteenth floor. But in 1938, a window washer's safety belt broke, and he plunged to his death—from the thirteenth floor.

They mentioned a woman rushing upstairs from the thirteenth to the fourteenth floor immediately after the shooting. During her interrogation in New York City, Miss Dove stated that she fled upstairs. But did she eventually die by her own hand, as described in the séance? We have not been able to find out.

Hayes' number sixty-seven didn't seem to fit anywhere. The only possibility could be that aside from the dealers, bartenders, musicians, waiters, croupiers and the operators of the casino, there were sixty-seven people in the room. However, there is no way to verify this.

As for the name "Dominic," we could find no mention of it. However, that does not mean there was no "Dominic" involved somewhere in the incidents that took place.

In late 1924, just a few months before the hotel opened, a young woman was found slain on a "rock and coral" ledge near the golf course next to the hotel. She left a small child. Could the entity of a woman looking for her child have been the spirit of the slain woman seeking to communicate with her child after all these years? Is there walking among us today a person in his fifties who is being sought by a mother slain many years ago?

Whatever the business is that remains unfinished, and keeps the other spirits earthbound, still is a mystery. Possibly another séance will tell us more.

I asked Nancy why mediums can see ghosts and we can't.

She replied, "When laymen see an apparition, it is a spirit that has crossed back over into the world of the living. In order for our medium friends to have seen and heard what they did during the séance, they, as living beings, had to cross into the dimension of the spirit world."

Parapsychologists have established that entities, ghosts, apparitions, or what have you, tend to hang around, inhabit or haunt places where they encountered traumatic experiences during their lives. And there was much trauma in the old Miami Biltmore Hotel and the Coral Gables veterans' hospital.

ing, wherein the party experiencing the event alleges that information is being gained from outside sources by no known means and in a waking state, trance or dream state.

Ghost—An image of a person, known to be deceased.

> The spirit of the dead who stood in life before thee
> are again in death around thee, and
> their will shall overshadow thee; be still.
>
> Edgar Allan Poe

15

A Song And
Dance And Death

Encased in a plastic oxygen tent with an endless network of wires and tubes attached to her nearly lifeless body, she clung tenaciously to life—a fighter to the end. She was vaguely aware of an occasional technician moving like a ghostly white presence around her, adjusting tubes, needles and monitoring her vital signs. An officious, ramrod-straight head nurse entered the room followed by a staff doctor. They lifted up the transparent tent and looked at the occupant. Billie could barely make out the stitched insignia on the nurse's uniform pocket— Metropolitan Hospital, Intensive Care, Cardiac Division.

"Stop whispering, nurse. This patient is comatose —can't hear a word you're saying. Don't bother finding her a bed in the ward. She won't make it through the night." With a look of curt dismissal, the doctor turned abruptly and left the room.

Billie Holiday, affectionately known to her many fans as "Lady Day," Queen of New York City's night people, lay gasping for air as her failing heart labored to sustain her. The copper-complexioned beauty, now an unwholesome ashen-gray, watched through a mental fog as her vital forces ebbed with every drop of glucose solution that dripped into her bloodstream.

Her moist, brown, half-opened eyes moved slowly to the left corner of her visual field, where one of New York's finest sat sprawled in a tilted-back chair. The blue-uniformed city policeman was relaxing on the job. He cocked his silver-badged cap over his eyes, and his head nodded in a restless sleep. Billie's consciousness faded in and out—like scenes in an old movie. She was under house arrest—"illegal possession of narcotics," they called it.

She was too weak to contemplate escape, and too demoralized to care much one way or the other. Pictures of the past drifted through her mind like moths circling a flame. How had it come to this? She had fame, international recognition as this century's greatest blues singer. She was the undisputed Duchess of the Jazz World. Sure, she thought, maybe my childhood wasn't all roses, but Mama did the best she could. And later I had everything anybody'd ever want. How could something so right have gone so wrong?

Twelve-year-old Sadie Fagan and Clarence Holiday, aged fifteen years, became parents to Eleanora on April 7, 1915, and the little girl attended their wedding three years later. Eleanora, who would one day become known to the world as Billie Holiday or "Lady Day," was raised as a Catholic girl in a Baptist world in the black slums of Baltimore, Maryland.

Eventually, her father, a skilled guitarist, went on the road with Fletcher Henderson's band, and Mama went to New York City to do housework for rich white folks. Billie stayed with her cousin, who was long on punishment and short on patience.

Alice Dean, a neighbor in their slum community, ran a brothel in Baltimore's red-light district. Billie would clean for Alice in exchange for "privileges." She'd listen to Alice's Victrola playing jazz records for hours, imitate the great blues singer Bessie Smith and sing to the inimitable sound of Louis Armstrong's famous horn. But when her cousin found out, Billie got a thrashing and was admonished not to become a "bad" girl. Alice said she'd whip Billie good if she ever caught her again.

Billie Holiday, the poignantly beautiful young Negro girl with skin the color of burnished copper, grew up the hard way in the slums and back alleys of the big city. Mama finally sprung her from a Catholic institution for wayward girls. She was sent there for closer supervision. The authorities had put Billie in the home when she was a little over ten years old—for being an underage victim of an attempted forcible rape. But things started looking up when Mama took her to live in New York City!

It was the early 1930's, and Billie's world throbbed to the sensuous Afro-American beat of jazz blues.

After a brief interlude as an underage and inadequate prostitute, Billie got a job singing at Pod and Jerry's place on West 133rd Street, and then the livin' was easy for Billie and Mama.

Billie sang to the likes of Tallulah Bankhead, Franchot Tone and Frederic March. The great and the not so great rubbed elbows at Pod and Jerry's place. But a hush fell over them as the lovely Negress with a big white gardenia in her hair stepped up to the mike and sang from the depths of her soul about the joy and the purgatory of being a woman— a black woman.

It was said that the unforgettable Billie Holiday had the greatest jazz voice of the century. Her voice could cry out the agony of human despair, reaching deep into the hearts of those who heard her weep the blues. It was as if she was trying to tell everyone who heard her sing, "This is the way it *feels,* because I've been there." And she *had* been there.

But things in New York were different from the old days. She was Miss Somebody now. Billie dressed like royalty and took care of her mama in grand style. Where did it go wrong? Was it that man Jimmy Monroe, whom she married in 1941, or that crazy "suicide song" she recorded in 1942, that jinxed her life? For it was in 1942 that she discovered Jimmy was into some drugs—hard stuff.

It didn't matter though, because the "Lady" loved her man. She sang the blues like never before—now they had two habits to support, Jimmy's and her own. Jimmy Monroe turned Billie Holiday on, in more than one way!

Sex goddess Lana Turner danced the Lindy and craved to hear Billie sing her favorites. "Gloomy Sunday," known as the "Suicide Song," was one of them. Lana would have her own share of tragedy in future years, but in the meantime she listened to Billie sing the blues, hour after hour.

After cutting "Gloomy Sunday," Billie's career and personal life plummeted to new all-time lows. T-men, Federal Narcotics Bureau people, busted Billie and Jimmy. Jimmy served time and Billie tried to kick the habit but failed over and over again in her attempts to do so. Heroin and "Gloomy Sunday" were winning the battle as agents dogged Billie's trail, arresting her time and time again. The great Billie Holiday, the world's foremost jazz-blues female vocalist, did hard time in the slammer. And she lost her man, too. The jinx of "Gloomy Sunday" hung on.

Billie's luck became increasingly bad. A convicted felon was not allowed to have a cabaret card. Without a card she could not work in the clubs. But plucky "Lady Day" did concerts and European tours to sustain herself financially.

Love came into Billie's life once again when she married Louis McKay, but the honeymoon feeling didn't last, for in 1956 Billie's brief respite from the jinx of heroin and "Gloomy Sunday" came to a halt. It was back to jail again on a narcotics violation.

And again, on June 12, 1959, federal agents arrested her on another charge of "illegal possession of narcotics." Five days later she was alone and under house arrest in the cold, sterile surroundings of New York City's Metropolitan Hospital. Billie Holiday, aged forty-four years, succumbed to death by lung congestion and heart failure. But were lung congestion and heart failure the true cause of her death, and the bad breaks leading up to it?

Billie Holiday, like a black Cinderella after the ball, should have lived happily ever after. What happened? Perhaps after refusing to heed the advice of her many advisers, she fell a victim to the incredible curse of Rezso Seress' fateful song, "Gloomy Sunday."

"Impossible," you say? Let the facts speak for themselves!

Rezso Seress wrote the music for "Gloomy Sunday" after experiencing the personal tragedy of a broken heart. Seress poured forth his endless despair and feeling of hopelessness for his lost love into the song in 1932. He met with little success in trying to publish it. His publishers sensed the all-consuming despair that was intrinsically part of the music. One letter of refusal said, "I don't think it would do anyone any good to hear a song like that."

Eventually, Seress published his own music. Then the bizarre became commonplace as each day a new batch of humanity did a macabre dance of death to the melancholy strains of "Gloomy Sunday."

GLOOMY SUNDAY*
by Laszlo Javor, Sam M. Lewis
and Rezso Seress

Sunday is gloomy, my hours are slumberless,
Dearest, the shadows I live with are numberless;
Little white flowers will never awaken you,
Not where the black coach of sorrow has taken you,
Angels have no thought of ever returning you.
Would they be angry if I thought of joining you,
Gloomy Sunday!

Gloomy is Sunday, with shadows I spend it all,
My heart and I have decided to end it all,
Soon there'll be candles and pray'rs that are sad,
I know, let them not weep, let them know
That I'm glad to go.
Death is no dream, for in death I'm caressing you.
With the last breath of my soul I'll be blessing you.
Gloomy Sunday!
Dreaming, I was only dreaming,
I wake and I find you asleep in the deep of my heart,
dear.
Dreaming, it was lonely dreaming;
I felt my heart melt when I dreamt that we two were
apart,
Far apart, far apart, far apart.
Darling, I hope that my dream never haunted you;
My heart is telling you how much I wanted you,
Gloomy Sunday.

A suicidal mania swept Europe as confirmed cases
of "Gloomy Sunday" madness reached epidemic proportions. The affliction infected the old and young
alike, both male and female, rich and poor.

No blame could be attached to a single issue. Yes,
the song and words were eerie, but there had been
stranger songs written that didn't compel men,
women and children to commit suicide. It is esti-
mated that hundreds became depressed and took
their own lives as a direct cause of "Gloomy Sunday"'s evil influence. More than a hundred people
died in one year, alone. The world became convinced
that the song bore an unholy curse. Fifteen different
countries banned its playing over the radio. Newspapers bore sensational headlines such as "KILLER
SONG STRIKES AGAIN," and the blame finally centered
on the man who gave birth to "Gloomy Sunday,"
Rezso Seress.

Families of victims discussed the advisability of
lawsuits against the composer. Their legal advisers
debated whether he could be prosecuted successfully,

and argued the extent of Rezso Seress' liability in the cases.

Witness the man in Hungary who, in full view of diners in a Budapest restaurant, requested the entertainers to play "Gloomy Sunday." Then he politely paid the bill, hailed a cab and shot himself to death.

Seress was not left unmarked by the enigma of "Gloomy Sunday." As the controversy increased, so did the sheet music sales. Buttressed by his dubious stroke of good fortune, Seress attempted to reconcile with his ex-sweetheart. He sent her a letter filled with tender entreaties.

A day later, she took poison and ended her young life. These words were scrawled on a tattered piece of paper found next to her dead body: "Gloomy Sunday."

But sales continued to climb. As many countries banned over-the-counter sales, black-market copies were illicitly sold. Not a week passed unmarred by "Gloomy Sunday"'s bizarre rampage of death.

Most typical are these two stories. A fourteen-year-old boy was cycling the streets of Rome. Upon hearing the deadly strains of "Gloomy Sunday" being sung by a street beggar, he parked his bike and emptied his pockets, giving the money to the singing beggar. Then he climbed the railing of a nearby bridge and plunged to his death in the murky waters below. Another case involved an eighty-year-old man, who flung himself from the window of a seven-story building after listening to the "Suicide Song" playing in his apartment.

When the instrumental version was first to be recorded in the United States by Hal Kemp (who himself died an early, tragic, accidental death), many of the musicians failed to show up for the recording session; over half were absent. So many weird, unexplainable things happened to abort the recording session that twenty-one different master

copies were attempted before a final one was successfully made.

One would think omission of the gloomy, depress-
ing words alone would have ended the parade of
senseless suicides. But it was Kemp's record that was
heard from an apartment window by a passing
London bobby, leading him inside to discover the
dead body of a woman. She had taken a drug overdose.

Awed and somewhat mystified by his eerie success
and notoriety, Rezso Seress declared, "I stand in the
midst of this deathly success as an accused man.
This fatal fame hurts me. I cried all the disappoint-
ments of my heart into this song, and it seems that
others with feelings like mine found their own hurt
in it ..."

Billie Holiday was not unaware of the effects of
"Gloomy Sunday" on people who came to hear her
sing. In her autobiographical book, *Lady Sings the
Blues*, she testifies to the "weird experiences" she
had. "There was a special character," she said, "who
had haunted the club for days, always asking for
'Strange Fruit' and 'Gloomy Sunday.'" She declared,
"I don't know why he wanted to hear either one.
He looked like 'Gloomy Sunday' to me." Perhaps it
was Billie being haunted, and not the club at all!

"Gloomy Sunday" isn't the only artistic work
stained with the crimson blood of its patrons. The
mid-eighteenth century had its bloodbath, too, when
a young man wrote a tragic love story that created
a sensation among the young people of that era.

Johann W. von Goethe, born in Frankfurt, Germany, in 1749, fell wildly in love with his best
friend's pretty fiancée, Charlotte Buff. But, as so often
happens, the twenty-five-year-old Johann was scorned
by his heart's desire. While nursing the nearly mortal
wounds of a broken heart, he wrote a popular novel
called *The Sorrows of Young Werther*. Into it, he
poured all his own tragedy and despair, basing the

hero and heroine, young Werther and Lotte, on his own wretched experience with love's caprices.

Goethe's novel was written in a few weeks. The tale is centered around a sensitive young man named Werther. He meets and falls in love with a beautiful young girl at a dance who is nothing less than an angel—a paragon of feminine virtue named Lotte. But Lotte is engaged to marry another, and even though he is constantly warned of the futility of desiring her, he persists and is eventually spurned when his attentions become obsessive.

Young Werther, in an "act of atonement," and as a release from what he considers a life without purpose, shoots himself. But his suicide attempt is bungled. The following morning, Werther is found bleeding his life away, still professing undying love for his perfidious Lotte.

The story of Young Werther was not as well written as Goethe's later works, such as the immortal *Faust*. What motivated young people of his generation to kill themselves in large numbers after reading his novel? It was as if a massive infection of suicidal mania had gripped the continent, taking the lives of many young European men and women.

The perpetrator, Goethe, was surprised and disturbed when reports of death's grim harvest reached his ears. Goethe had become a thinker in occult mysteries and later became fascinated with alchemy and science. After deliberating on the phenomena empirically, his answer to his accusers was that he considered the "curse associated with reading his novel to be caused by the dangerous side of his own personality," with which he believed the novel became impregnated, making it lethal reading material for disenchanted lovers.

Many of us have walked into a room and experienced a feeling of unexplainable evil. Others have held certain objects that seemed to emanate an aura of death. Psychometrists can "read" a piece of jewelry or clothing, telling the wearer many personal details about his or her life. Perhaps Goethe was correct—words (or music) can hold the magical spell of doom.

Sometimes it's not the written words of music that are permeated with an evil force, but rather where the song is played! The Ryman Building, located in downtown Nashville, was the center of repeated tragedies for a number of years.

"When's it all going to end?" said a despairing Herb Shucher, national promotion director for a company called Star Records. Mr. Shucher's query reflected a question on the lips of millions of country and western music fans throughout the nation.

An ever-growing number of tragedies has plagued Grand Ole Opry troopers. Many have experienced great personal trials and losses. A little more than a decade has seen eleven Opry luminaries killed by violence. And when they died, they took others with them—business associates, relatives and colleagues. The combined death toll has climbed to thirty-five. Country music stars have burned to death, have suffered beatings, robberies and murder by gunfire, have become victims of automobile and airplane accidents and have succumbed to tragedies related to alcohol and drugs.

Little wonder there has been talk of an "Opry Jinx" or hex that stalks the Opry performers as they appear under the floodlights. Some say the "curse" is a life-style risk based on percentages; after all, when you travel a hundred thousand miles or more each year in planes and automobiles, the odds are against you.

The monstrous, senseless 1973 murders of country and western music's "Stringbean" Akeman (the beloved comic of *Hee-Haw* television fame) and his wife of twenty-five years are among the most heinous deaths attributed to the Nashville jinx. Robbers and soon-to-be killers hid and waylaid the Akemans when they returned from a Grand Ole Opry performance. They entered the small but cozy Akeman home through the back door. As "Stringbean" entered the front door, he was shot to death. Mrs. Akeman, fore-warned by the shots that killed her husband, fled across the yard. She received three head wounds from flying bullets as the killers pursued and caught her. She was found lying face down in the grass. The killers failed to find the cache of money totaling $2,200 that Mrs. Akeman had attached to her bra in a tobacco sack. Mr. Akeman's cash trove of $3,500, which was hidden in a secret pocket of his bib over-alls, was also overlooked. The murderers made good their escape—temporarily—in the Akeman family's blue Ford station wagon.

Sixteen days after the Akeman murders, Jimmy Widener, Opry star Hank Snow's personal friend and a guitar-strumming member of Snow's "Rainbow Ranch Boys," along with Jimmy's companion, the widow of a deceased Nashville celebrity, were both dead—robbed, shot and dumped in a muddy puddle in one of Nashville's back alleys.

The famous Hank Snow identified Widener's body. He was quoted as saying, "First it was String-bean, a good guy. Now it's Jimmy, one helluva nice guy. I wonder when it's going to stop."

Hank had good reason to wonder when the rampage of death would cease, for he had watched the death toll mount. Snow had attended the graveside services of many men and women associated with country music, with whom he had worked and whom he once called "friend."

Ira Louvin and his wife, both country music entertainers, were killed in 1965, in a fatal, head-on automobile crash. The accident took the lives of two companions and the oncoming vehicle's occupants as well. A year earlier, in 1964, Jim Reeves, the Opry celebrity who recorded such all-time country hits as "Bimbo" and "He'll Have to Go," along with his accompanist, Dean Manuel, perished in a plane crash. The year 1963 saw four prominent personalities of country music dead in a similar accident. Cowboy Copas, Patsy Cline, Randy Hayes and Hawkshaw

Hawkins were all killed when their private plane slammed into a mountain. Ironically, Jack Anglin, a tenor in Nashville's famous "Johnny and Jack" singing duo, died en route to the funeral of Patsy Cline, when his car went out of control and struck a tree.

Very shortly thereafter, "Texas Ruby" Fox, a former Grand Ole Opry singer, died of fumes inhaled when her mobile home burned. Fourteen people perished in Opryland during a three-year period alone. Their only apparent connection was their work in country and western music, and—the Grand Ole Opry.

Other artists escaped death but were hounded nonetheless by similar mysterious happenings.

The year 1964 ended the dazzling career of superstar Jim Reeves in a plane crash, and very nearly brought down the curtain on a Grand Ole Opry legend and a future country and western luminary.

If a psychic premonition of impending disaster had not forewarned Jack Greene, the great Ernest Tubb and a busload of Opryland's finest musicians might all have fallen victim to the lethal "Opry Jinx."

Jack Greene, later to become known as the "Jolly Greene Giant," takes his premonitions seriously. While traveling on the road with Ernest Tubb and the boys as a drummer and relief bus driver, he was overcome by a feeling of uneasiness. Johnny Wiggins was driving but Jack insisted on taking the wheel. Less than five minutes later, as the bus ascended a hilltop, two semi-tractor-trailers on a double-lane road, driving full throttle side by side, met Jack Greene and his passengers—head on! Had he not intuitively pulled off the road seconds before meeting the trucks, a disaster would no doubt have claimed the lives of everyone aboard. Jack Greene survived to give the country and western music world some of its greatest songs. "There Goes My Everything" was Jack's single greatest smash hit and his songs continue to make number one on hit-parade charts.

Another "almost gotcha" is Hank Williams, Jr. His father, the late Hank Williams, Sr., died in 1953, a victim of the Opry life-style: After a string of hectic one-night gigs, he was found dead in the back seat of his car. In 1975, singer Hank, Jr., a celebrity in his own right, fell five hundred feet while scaling a Montana mountain. His injuries were gruesome, but after a nip and tuck fight for life, he eventually recovered. Hank looked like a latter-day Humpty Dumpty—his head was broken open and his forehead smashed. He was also minus his teeth and a good part of his nose, but he survived. Wavering on the critical list for three days, Williams lost forty-five pounds in a fifteen-day period. Hank Williams, Jr., was not only plagued by physical suffering; the jinx also extended to his personal life. He was divorced twice and his mother died in November 1975, three months after his near-fatal mountain-climbing accident.

Was there really an "Opry Jinx," or was the surging tidal wave of death and misery merely representative of a fast-moving life-style?

Red Foley died on October 19, 1968. He was the Opry entertainer who helped make Christian spiritual songs acceptable as popular music. Songs such as "Peace in the Valley," "Just a Closer Walk with Thee" and "Steal Away" made gospel music acceptable entertainment in Las Vegas nightclubs. Slot machines stopped and all eyes turned to hear Red sing hope-filled gospel messages of redemption and life after death with his Lord and Savior. But Red had a show-business-related problem—he drank heavily. His streak of bad luck can't be attributed entirely to his life-style or bad habits. For instance, Red's first wife died in childbirth, and his beloved second wife took her own life. Foley attempted suicide by taking a large quantity of sleeping pills in 1952, but survived to die of lung congestion in 1968. He was well liked and the music industry marked his passing with deep mourning. Some attributed his death to words he had said to them many times, "I'm my own worst enemy." However, an examination of the facts show that his self-defeating attitude and serious drinking started after a run of bad luck that would have driven a saint to drink!

One observer of the "Opry Jinx," a country and western star, theorized: "Take a guy who's a comedian. Something funny happens to him and everybody thinks it's natural. He's a funny guy and funny things happen to him, and so the comedian lives up to his role. Why then are fans so surprised when the sad things we sing about happen to us more often than normal?"

The beautiful blonde country and western singer Tammy Wynette must carry a lucky rabbit's foot, or perhaps a bushel of four-leaf clovers. She has survived two marriages, the burning of her Nashville home in 1976, a hysterectomy, kidney surgery and a gall-bladder operation. Tammy's doctors also prescribed hospital rest when she suffered from exhaustion on several occasions. Many times she has packed the theater and gone on with the show in spite of being in agonizing pain.

Near tragedy struck Tammy's life again during the first week of October 1978, when she was abducted from a shopping-center parking lot in Nashville. After several terrifying hours, the kidnappers released the bruised and bloodied singer. As of this writing no motive has been offered for the crime, nor have the culprits been caught. Periodically she still receives threatening letters from her kidnappers. Could it have been a mere coincidence, or does the jinx live on?

Is it possible that the negative happenings sung about continually by old-timers of country music could enter the subconscious of the entertainers, programing them for death, heartache and violence?

The truth might very well lie somewhere among the three possibilities: life-style, "programed misery," and—the "Opry Jinx."

> Hark! They whisper: angels say,
> brother spirit, come away!
> What is this absorbs me quite?
> Steals my senses, shuts my sight,
> drowns my spirit, draws my breath?
> Tell me, my soul, can this be death?
> Alexander Pope

16

The Curse on
James Dean's Death Car

The descending sun was closing the gap on the ridge atop the Mountains of the Devil as the silver-gray streak raced westward. It was as if the thirteen hundred pounds of aluminum and steel had been flung from some giant catapult. The sixteen-inch tires clung to the white concrete two-lane highway leaving behind an infinitesimal amount of rubber with each revolution. There was no deviation from the track . . . The vehicle and the road were made for each other as were the car and its driver. They were as one—part of each other. The scream of the Porsche's engine ripped apart the silence of Antelope Valley. Ahead, a strange and fateful rendezvous with destiny awaited the car and its driver.

James Bryan Dean was born February 8, 1931, at Marion, Indiana. When he was six, he moved with his parents to California. During the ninth year of his life his mother died, and young Jimmy never found out quite why. He returned to Indiana to be raised by an aunt and uncle, Ortense and Marcus Winslow.

After graduating from high school in 1949, James Dean returned to California where he enrolled in Santa Monica City College. There, he became active in the drama department. After one semester, he transferred to U.C.L.A., where he majored in pre-law and minored in theater arts. After the first year and several acting jobs on television, including a Pepsi-Cola commercial, he dropped out of school to become a full-time actor—when he could find work. But acting parts did come, bit parts at first but eventually *East of Eden, Rebel Without a Cause,* and *Giant.*

As his acting career soared, so did Dean's taste in cars. He had grown up on motorbikes, motorcycles and flivvers. His first true sports car was a red MG-TD. His favorite pastime with the MG was to lower the top, fold the windshield forward and race along back roads at night, "chasing the moon." Then the racing bug bit him.

He entered his first race in April 1955, driving his newly purchased Porsche Speedster at Palm Springs. His racing career began promisingly. In that first race, he won a first place in the amateur division and took a third in the professional class.

Less than a month later he entered the Bakersfield National Sports Car Races and drove to a first in his class. At Santa Barbara four weeks later he was again a winner.

After that race, Dean spent most of the summer in west Texas near the town of Marfa for the filming of *Giant,* which co-starred Elizabeth Taylor and Rock Hudson. Warner Brothers studio refused to allow their hottest property to race during the film's production. Filmmaker George Stevens had rented a Chevrolet convertible for Dean. But when he saw how his star was racing around the countryside in it, the director gave the car back to the rental agency.

On completion of the filming, James Dean returned to Los Angeles. A small import sports-car company,

Competition Motors,* had a new 1955 Porsche Spyder and offered it at $6,900. The Spyder was one of the hottest vehicles racing the sports-car circuits, and it didn't take the young actor long to hear about the car.

He sold his $3,700 Porsche Speedster and bought the Spyder, after driving it once around the block. Jimmy put a condition on his purchase, however. He would buy the machine only if one of the company's mechanics, Rolf Wuetherich, would personally prepare the Spyder and accompany the car as its mechanic to all races. Rolf, who had served in the Luftwaffe, agreed. Although he was only twenty-eight, Rolf was considered to be one of the best Porsche mechanics on the West Coast. Thus, the first move toward the rendezvous with destiny was taken.

"There was something strange about the car. It gave me an eerie feeling whenever I got near it," said George Barris, one of California's leading car designers. "He dropped the car off at my shop on a Tuesday morning to have a racing stripe painted on it and said that he would pick it up that afternoon. He was planning to drive it on the following Saturday, October 1, 1955, in the races at Salinas, the town where his first big movie, *East of Eden*, took place.

"I've driven and customized thousands of cars," continued Barris, "but never did I ever encounter one that gave off such a weird feeling of impending doom. I had known Jimmie since I met him on the set of *Rebel Without a Cause*. I worked on his other cars, including the Speedster, but none gave me that feeling like something's going to happen."

I asked George if anyone else had any unusual feelings about the Spyder.

"Several of his other friends picked up the same

---

*Later to become known as Volkswagen Pacific.

vibes," he said. "Ursula Andress and Alec Guiness were two of them."

"Jimmie dropped by my house with the car right after he bought it. He really was proud of it," said Ms. Andress. "He bought it as a present for himself after finishing his third picture. I told him that the car gave me a bad feeling. Laughing, he promised to be careful and said good-bye. I knew that I would never see him again."

Alec Guiness told Dean, "If you're smart, you'll get rid of that car."

Nick Adams, another friend of the rising young superstar, who played "Johnny Yuma" in the television series *The Rebel*, also felt funny about the Porsche. "When I told him," said Adams, "he said that his death in a speeding car was destined."

Just before they left, Jimmy's uncle, Charlie Nolan, told his nephew, "Jim, be careful. You're sitting on a bomb."

Dean was wearing dungarees and a white T-shirt when he wheeled the "Little Bastard," as he called the silver-gray Spyder, onto Ventura Boulevard and north out of Los Angeles. Weutherich was riding with him. Two friends were following in Jimmie's Ford station wagon towing a trailer. They were his actor friend Bill Hickman and Stan Roth, a photographer for *Colliers* magazine who was planning to do a picture story on Dean at the Salinas races the next day. Originally, the Porsche was to be trailered to Salinas, but Dean wanted to get in all the time he could behind the wheel prior to the race. They stopped for gas and then sped north on Highway 99 with the Ford following behind.

As the two vehicles were approaching Bakersfield, Donald Gene Turnupseed, a California Polytechnic student, was driving home for the weekend in his older-model black and white Ford sedan. Turnupseed, who like Dean was twenty-four, had hoped to arrive in Tulare, his hometown, by dark. The second round of events leading to the preordained rendezvous with destiny was taking place.

The sun was reaching further to the west in the cloudless California sky as the Porsche turned off U.S. 99 and headed west on Route 466.*

Twenty-six miles later, Dean slowed down for the hamlet of Lost Hills which stands just west of where Interstate 5 passes under Route 46. Back in 1955, however, the Interstate was but a pencil line on a highway engineer's map.

West of Lost Hills, the highway was in a straight line without a curve for twelve miles across the yellowish-gold-colored Antelope Plain. It is not known what speed Dean's car attained along the straightaway, although it had a capability in excess of one hundred and fifty miles per hour.

Sixty miles to the west, Turnupseed had just left Paso Robles and was driving east on Route 466. Driving conditions were ideal all along the two-lane highway. There was no indication of what fate had in store.

The silver-gray Spyder sped on as though it were trying to catch the sun. Ahead, barely visible through the haze, lay the Diablo Range—the Mountains of the Devil.

Oil rigs resembling voracious prehistoric monsters dotted the landscape. Tractors working the fields kicked up smoke-screen trails of brown dust. Desert pines were scattered here and there. The whitish-gray roadway unfolded before the Porsche as though it were a supersonic conveyor belt. A sign with an arrow flashed by: "DEVIL'S DEN TEN MILES." Like giant dunes in a desert, the Diablo Range loomed larger.

Puffing one Chesterfield king after another, Dean pressed heavily on the gas pedal, occasionally removing his eyes from the road ahead to glance at the tachometer.

---

*Today, Route 466 is designated as State Highway 46.

As they approached Blackwell's Corner, a two-structure settlement where 466 intersected 33, something caused James Dean to take his eyes from the road. He caught a glimpse of an object that only a lover of exotic motorcars would notice. He slowed down and wheeled into the parking lot of the combination gas station, grocery store, restaurant and 3.2 beer joint. The Spyder stopped alongside the gray Mercedes-Benz 300 SL gull-wing sports car parked in the lot. The predestined encounter with fate was coming closer, for Donald Turnupseed's black and white car was still moving east on 466.

Lance Reventlow, owner of the Mercedes, and son of Woolworth heiress Barbara Hutton, came out when he saw the Spyder. Reventlow, who was also heading for the races at Salinas, would one day become a competition sports-car racer of renown. The two racing-machine owners discussed cars and mutual acquaintances for several minutes until Roth and Hickman caught up in the station wagon. They made plans to meet for dinner that night in Paso Robles. Dean and Wuetherich climbed into the Porsche. As he was about to start up the engine, Dean hesitated, got out of the car, went into the store and bought a six-pack of beer. The delay guaranteed the rendezvous with destiny, for Donald Turnupseed's black and white Ford sedan was still moving eastward along 466.

The Spyder's speedometer was hovering at eighty-five. The driver's hair flew straight back in the wind as the hot air swooshed over the windscreen. The regular windshield had been replaced by a frameless glass racing screen.

Mexican laborers working the vineyards and farmlands along 466 turned their heads lazily in wonderment to see what was causing the banshee-like scream that echoed across the countryside. The silver-gray streak flashed past in a blur.

Wuetherich, the mechanic, reached behind his seat for Dean's red jacket, which he donned. The station wagon was now barely a speck far back on the horizon. The Spyder's steering wheel was performing just as its driver wanted it to. With his hands on the wheel, his body pressed into the bucket seat, his right foot on the accelerator and his brain on the same wavelength as the four-cam 110-horsepower engine roaring under the rear-deck lid, James Dean and the Porsche Spyder, the "Little Bastard," had become part of each other. They were one and the same.

The tach needle didn't waiver as the vehicle raced up the grade toward Polonio Pass, which led Route 466 through the Devil's Range.* The only waiver on the speedometer was when the driver pressed harder on the gas pedal, hurling the machine ahead even faster than eighty-five miles per hour.

Donald Turnupseed's Ford had passed through the town of Shandon and was nearing Cholame, a little burg consisting of a gas station, restaurant and post office. Its population—five. Fate waited—now only minutes away.

Dean held the throttle at eighty-five as the Spyder sped down the long Antelope Grade toward where 466 meets 41, which connects that junction with Tulare to the northeast. The sun was getting lower, turning the whitish-gray color of the concrete roadway to a cadaver gray. Five miles now separated the two cars—five miles to infinity.

The sun, moving lower, was just beginning to cause a glare through the Porsche's windscreen. There were no visors, for the Spyder was a racing machine.

Turnupseed was passing through Cholame, still another mile away from the turnoff of 466 onto 41.

Dean was nearing the bottom of Antelope Grade. The road ahead was straight and empty. One hundred and eighty miles to the south it was the peak rush hour on Los Angeles freeways. Traffic there,

---

*The range is actually called the Diablo Range. Diablo is Spanish for "devil."

under a pall of smog suspended over the city, was bumper to bumper. Horns blew as temperatures and tempers soared. But east of Cholame, 466 was empty as far as the driver of the Spyder could see. The air above was clear. It was great to be alive—free like a bird. With the wind in his face and the steady drone of a powerful unfaltering engine and a car that responded to his every whim, James Dean had the ultimate in motoring.

Around three minutes to six, the Spyder and the Ford sedan came in view of each other. Dean's foot remained steady on the accelerator. The speedometer still read eighty-five. The black and white Ford moved slowly across the center line of the roadway. Turnupseed was getting ready to make his left turn onto 41 at the Y-shaped intersection. The distance between the two cars was diminishing fast.

"That car's coming into our lane!" screamed Dean. "That guy's got to stop!"

Turnupseed realized what was about to happen. He couldn't decide whether to accelerate and try to beat the oncoming Porsche across the intersection, or to swerve back to the east-bound lane in order to avoid contact with the Spyder. Should he stop, go ahead or swerve back to the right? He panicked and hit the brakes. It was too late. The rendezvous with doom had to take place.

There was an explosion of shattering metal and flying glass as the Porsche's fifteen hundred pounds of aluminum and steel hurled into the Ford. Perhaps, if Turnupseed had swerved back into the east-bound lane, or accelerated through the intersection . . . Maybe, if Dean had been driving within the speed limit, or if he had accelerated through the intersection—or if he hadn't gone back for the six-pack of beer . . . Maybe . . . perhaps . . . maybe . . .

By six o'clock, quiet once again reigned above the San Andreas Fault, at the junction of Routes 466 and 41.

Turnupseed lay across the front seat of his car

with head and facial lacerations. Rolf Wuetherich lay on the ground twenty feet from the wreck with a fractured jaw, a broken leg and internal injuries.

The Porsche, crumpled like a pack of cigarettes, was nearly torn in two. The steering wheel and driver's seat were shoved so far over that the car appeared to be right-hand-driven. James Bryan Dean, his neck broken and his body shattered and crumpled like the silver-gray Spyder which, only seconds before, he had been a part of, lay slung over the passenger-side door. A new legend had been born.

By the time the ambulance, involved in an accident itself en route, arrived at the Paso Robles War Memorial Hospital, Rolf had regained consciousness. An intern climbed inside the van of the ambulance and looked at Jimmie Dean. The actor was on the lower stretcher. Rolf watched as the medic examined the young man who had made the transition from superstar to legend in an instant. The blood-covered Dean was limp. His arms and legs stuck out at weird angles. From the angle of his head, the intern knew that Dean's neck had snapped. In the emergency room, a doctor pronounced him dead.

Turnupseed, who was driven to the hospital in a police car, suffered a bloody forehead and lacerated nose. He was treated and released.

Mechanic Wuetherich would be hospitalized for many months, before recovering and returning to Germany, where he went back to work at the Porsche factory.

Word of James Dean's death hit the movie colony like a bomb. Elizabeth Taylor and several members of the *Giant* company were in the screening room looking at rushes when the phone rang. Miss Taylor later recalled: "I heard George Stevens [the director] answer it and say, 'Oh, God! No, when? Are you sure it was him?' He hung up the phone, stopped the projector, and turned on the lights. He turned to us and said, 'I've just been told the news that Jimmie Dean has been killed.'"

It was later determined that the Spyder's average speed between 3:30 p.m., when Dean was given a speeding ticket by trooper Otie Hunter on the Grapevine Grade outside of Bakersfield, and the time of the accident at 5:59 p.m., allowing for the fifteen-minute stop at Blackwell's Corner, had to be eighty-six miles per hour.

A grand jury hearing the case made no indictments or charges. Their verdict was accidental death.

But was the sudden demise of James Byran Dean accidental? We cannot help but wonder when we recall the interview with George Barris in Los Angeles, and how the custom automobile designer told of the feeling he had about the Porsche Spyder when Dean brought it in for the racing stripe. And then, too, there were the others: Alec Guiness; Ursula Andress; Jimmie's uncle, Charles Nolan; and Nick Adams.

Could the 1955 silver-gray Porsche Spyder that streaked across the California countryside on September 30, 1955, carrying James Dean to his death, have had something evil in its background? Could something possibly have happened at the Porsche factory in Germany—or maybe aboard the ship that transported the car to the United States? Or could it be that periodically a car might leave the factory carrying with it a jinx?

Many people have attributed Dean's death to his driving habits. Yet those who had seen him race called him a good driver with great potential. Let's look at the facts concerning the "Little Bastard," and how it affected others besides Jimmie Dean.

George Barris, the friend of James Dean's who got an eerie feeling every time he went near the car, bought the wreck from the insurance underwriters for $2,500. "It was a rare car," he said, "and components for that model were not easy to come by, so I bought it for parts. Now I wish that I'd sent it to the junkyard and had it shredded."

"Why?" I asked the master car designer.

"After the wreck arrived back at my garage, some of my mechanics were unloading it from a truck when suddenly the car slipped and fell on one of them, breaking both his legs.

"Then I sold the engine of Jimmie's car to Dr. Troy McHenry, a Beverly Hills physician whose hobby was racing sports cars. Another physician, Dr. William F. Eschrid of Burbank, bought the drive train [the transmission, etc.].

"Both doctors were preparing their cars for a race to be held at the Pomona Fair Grounds on October 24, 1956. After that race I knew the car carried a curse."

Barris shifted uneasily in his chair as I pumped him for more information.

"Well, in driving that race at Pomona, Dr. McHenry—who installed Dean's engine in his car; it was the first time he raced with that engine—was killed when his car went out of control and crashed into a tree.

"Dr. Eschrid, who was using Dean's drive train for the first time in that same race, was seriously injured when his car rolled over. Dr. Eschrid said later that he didn't have any idea what happened—just that when he went into a curve, the car suddenly locked on him and rolled over."

"I can understand why you wanted to have the car destroyed," commented Nancy.

"Yeah, it was really becoming a burden to me. Everybody was coming to my lot to look at the wreck. One kid, while trying to steal the steering wheel for a souvenir, slipped and ripped his arm open on a piece of jagged metal. And someone else got hurt trying to rip out a piece of bloodstained upholstery. It seemed like every Dean fan in the country came to see the car."

Barris went on to tell how he sold the car's two undamaged heavy-duty racing tires to a sports-car buff. "I didn't want to sell them, for fear that something might happen, but the young man insisted.

"Less than a week later, he called me and said that he'd run off the road and nearly wrecked his car when the two tires from the Dean car blew out simultaneously. I examined both of the tires and couldn't find any defects or faults in either one.

"After that," continued Barris, "I decided that I would just put the car away in one of my storage garages where it couldn't harm anyone else.

"However, it wasn't long afterward that the California Highway Patrol approached me. They wanted to use the car in a traveling safety exhibit. So I decided to let them use it, figuring that maybe it could begin saving lives instead of taking them. I welded all of the pieces together so the car wouldn't fall apart."

But Barris was wrong about the car saving lives instead of taking them. After being shown at two exhibits without incident, it was taken to Fresno one evening to be displayed on the following day. There it was stored for the night in a Highway Patrol garage. Four hours later, the garage was a mass of flames, which destroyed it and the adjacent building. Every vehicle in the garage was destroyed—except the Porsche Spyder. The paint on it was slightly scorched.

The Dean car was then taken to Sacramento where it was put on exhibit. While a class of high-school students was gathered around it, the car fell off its display pedestal, breaking a teen-age bystander's hip.

Several weeks later, George Barkuis, a State of California employee, was transporting the Spyder to Salinas on a flatbed truck. (Salinas was Dean's destination at the time he was killed.) But, possibly, something near Salinas influenced the curse of James Dean's car, for George Barkuis, like Dean, never reached that town. Barkuis lost control of the truck and was thrown from the cab. The Porsche wreck tore loose from the truck's bed and came crashing down on Barkuis—killing him instantly.

Two years later near Oakland, the Porsche broke

in two and fell from a truck onto the freeway, causing an accident.

In 1958, the truck carrying the Dean car was parked on a hill in Oregon. The truck's emergency brake slipped, causing the truck to crash through a store window. Fortunately, no one was injured in that mishap.

In 1959, while the Porsche was on display in New Orleans, it suddenly broke into eleven pieces while sitting on its display stand. When Barris received it back, he could find no cause for the car's coming apart by itself.

And other things have happened. The curse began to extend itself to those indirectly concerned with the death car and its driver. Nick Adams, who substituted his own voice for Dean's in several scenes in *Giant*, died from an overdose of paraldehyde in 1968.

Lance Reventlow, whose 300-SL Mercedes drew Dean's attention at Blackwell's Corner and delayed Dean just long enough, went on to a successful racing career. But in a manner similar to James Dean's movie career, Reventlow's driving career was cut short before its prime when the Woolworth heir died in a plane crash.

Sal Mineo, who was Dean's main supporting actor in *Rebel Without a Cause* and an off-screen personal friend, was found stabbed to death in 1976.

Rolf Wuetherich, Dean's mechanic, is still alive. He did not escape the curse of the death car, however. In 1968, he was sentenced to life imprisonment for the murder of his wife. All he offered for his defense at his trial was a plea of insanity.

But what about the death car itself, after all these years? In 1960, the Porsche was loaned to the Florida Highway Patrol for a safety exhibit in Miami. After the showing, the car was crated up, loaded on a truck and sent on its way back to Los Angeles. Barris awaited its arrival, for the National Safety Council wanted to put it on display. After a week, the car still hadn't arrived. Barris called Miami and was told that the Porsche was definitely on its way. But James Dean's car never arrived. Somewhere between Miami and Los Angeles it vanished without a trace, never to be seen again . . .

GLOSSARY

Apparitions of living persons—Sometimes known as an "etheric double"; one sees a physical representation of someone known to be in a distant place.

Apparitions of the dead—An individual known to be physically dead appears in solid form to percipient; in most cases, a relative of the perceiver.

Clairaudience—Seeing and hearing events, or having knowledge of same, outside the range of physical visual perception.

Clairsentience—Often used to include gifts of clairvoyance, clairaudience and other ESP modalities combined.

Clairvoyance (ESP)—Having knowledge of objects, events or persons not within visual sight.

"Cold Spot"—A pervasive localized chill associated with hauntings, theorized by some parapsychologists to be caused by a drain on thermal energy and body heat which is used by disembodied entities to move objects or to become visible.

Dematerialization—Physical objects disappear quite rapidly.

Demons—Thought by many occultists to be cohorts of the biblical being, Satan, a fallen angel. Demons, allegedly, can take the form of animals or obsess and possess human beings. They can appear as male or female, as great beauties or horrible monsters.

"Earthbound"—A word applied to returned spirits who for reasons unknown remain attached to their earthly environment and stay relatively innocuous, as long as they are left to enjoy their long-accustomed habitats.

Extrasensory perception (ESP)—A psychic happening, wherein the party experiencing the event alleges that information is being sent through outside sources, by no known sensory channel, in a waking state, trance or dream state.

Ghost—An image of a person, known to be deceased, that appears to the living. This does not include occurrences of bilocation, out-of-body experiences or astral projection.

Hauntings—The return of personalities from beyond physical death, known to be seen in certain predictable locations.

"Hot spot"—A term used loosely to denote any area of concentrated psychic energy that can be perceived by an individual sensitive to such emanations.

Levitation—The object or person rises into the air by no obvious physical means.

Materialization—Forms or objects, which previously had no physical presence, suddenly become visible in solid form.

Medium—One who sees or communicates with disembodied personalities, or allows him- or herself to become a temporary channel for such entities to communicate through.

Out-of-the-Body Projection (OOBP)—Consciousness separates from the physical body and gains knowledge of distant places or happenings.

Paranormal—An abnormal occurrence that cannot be explained scientifically.

Parapsychology—The scientific study of abnormal phenomena, or the unexplainable.

Poltergeist—A noisy ghost. Objects are moved, sometimes broken; appears in most cases to be caused by a living entity experiencing emotional upheaval. Agent is not aware that he is creating phenomena.

Precognition (ESP)—Awareness of events to happen in future time that cannot be inferred from present knowledge. Predictions of things to occur.

Psychic Healing—When an illness or disability disappears without the aid of medicaments.

Psychic Surgery—When diseased tissue is removed from the physical body without the use of surgical instruments.

Psychokinesis (PK)—The movement of physical objects minus a visible causative agent, for which there is no known explanation.

Psychometry—Reading of objects by using ESP. Knowing about a person by examining a personal belonging of the person.

Radiesthesia—Dowsing, finding water or other precious substances through use of ESP faculties.

Reincarnation—A survival of personality after death, reborn in another human being.

Retrocognition (ESP)—Knowledge of past events; insight into past happenings beyond range of the normal.

Spirit Photography—Appearance of images of the dead on photographic plates of persons not present when photo was taken.

Spirit Possession—A condition where a living person appears to be taken over by a disembodied entity that is not, in every case, human.

Survival Phenomena—Events caused by disembodied personalities, or beings, ghosts, hauntings, etc.

Telekinesis—Stationary object movement without physical force being exerted.

Telepathy (ESP)—One individual receives another individual's emotional state, or thought.

Teleportation—"Apports." Objects are moved over great distances, or through physical objects.

Thoughtography—Images are produced on unexposed film by thought projection alone.

BIBLIOGRAPHY
Books

Ald, R., *The Case for an Afterlife*. New York: Lancer Books, 1968.

Anderson, J., *The Haunting of America*. Boston: Houghton, 1975.

Arthur, S.C., *Old New Orleans*. New Orleans: Harmanson, 1937.

Barden, D., *Ghosts and Hauntings*. New York: Taplinger, Inc., 1965.

Barker, J.C., *Scared To Death*. New York: Dell, 1968.

Barris & Scagnett, *Cars of the Stars*. Middle Village: J. David Publishing, 1974.

Baskin, W., *The Sorcerer's Handbook*. London: Peter Owen, 1974.

Brandon, J., *Weird America*. New York: Dutton, 1978.

Burger, R., *Alcatraz*. San Francisco: Cameron, 1974.

Carrington, H., *Haunted People*. New York: Dutton, 1951.

Colby, C.B., *Strangely Enough*. New York: Popular Library, 1959.

Dingwall, E.J., *The Unknown—Is it Nearer?* New York: Signet, 1956.

Dufty, W., *Lady Sings the Blues*. New York: Lancer, 1956.

Ebon, M., *Communicating With the Dead*. New York: Signet, 1968. *The Evidence for Life After Death*. New York: Signet, 1977. *True Experiences With Ghosts*. New

York: New American Library, 1968. *They Knew the Unknown*. New York: Signet, 1971.

Fate, *Stranger than Strange* (A compilation by Editors of Best of Fate Magazine). Highland Park, Ill.: Clark Pub. Co., 1966.

Feckles, E.V., *Willie Speak Out—The Psychic World of Abraham Lincoln*. St. Paul, Minn.: Llewellyn, 1977.

Fodor, N., *Between Two Worlds*. Englewood Cliffs, N.J.: Parker, 1964. *Encyclopedia of Psychic Science*. Secaucus, N.J.: Citadel, 1974.

Garrett, E.J., *Adventures in the Supernormal*. New York: Paperback Library, 1949.

Gentry, L., *A History & Encyclopedia of Country, Western, and Gospel Music*, 1969.

Hayes, P., *Know Yourself*. Miami: 1974.

Herndon, V., *James Dean* (*A Short Life*). New York: Doubleday, 1975.

Hibbert, C., *The Roots of Evil*. Boston: Little, Brown, 1963.

Hill, D., *The History of Ghosts, Vampires and Werewolves*. Baltimore: Ottenheimer, 1970. *The Supernatural*. London: Aldous Books, 1965.

Hollaran, C.R., *Meet the Stars of Country Music*. Nashville: Aurora Pub., Inc., 1977.

Holzer, H., *Ghosts of the Golden West*. New York: Ace, 1968. *Yankee Ghosts*. New York: Ace, 1966. *The Ghosts That Walk Washington*. New York: Ballantine, 1971. *Beyond This Life*. New York: Bobbs-Merrill, 1969. *Psychic Investigator*. New York: Popular Library, 1968. *Ghost Hunter*. New York: Ace, 1963.

Howard, C., *Six Against the Rock*. New York: Dial, 1977.

Huggett, R., *Supernatural on Stage*. New York: Taplinger, 1975.

Hurwood, B.J., *Strange Lives*. New York: Popular Library, 1966.

Ingram, M.V., *Authenticated History of the Bell Witch*. Rare Book Reprints, 1961.

Kleiner, D., *The Ghost Who Danced with Kim Novak*. New York: Ace, 1969.

Kobler, J., *Capone*. New York: Putnam, 1971.

Langdon-Davies, J., *The Unknown—Is It Nearer?* New York: Signet, 1956.

Lee, M.D., *Virginia Ghosts*. Berryville, Va.: Virginia Book Co., 1966.

Lewis, V.A., *History of the Battle of Point Pleasant*. Harrisburg, Va.: C. U. Carrier Co., 1909.

Macklin, J., *The Enigma of the Unknown*. New York: Ace 1967. *Brotherhood of the Strange*. New York: Ace, 1972. *Prelude to Nightmare*. New York: Ace, 1970. *Journey Beyond the Grave*, New York: Ace, 1970. *Caravan of the Occult*. New York: Ace, 1971. *Passport to the Unknown*. New York: Ace, 1968. *A Look Through Secret Doors*. New York: Ace, 1969.

McConnaughey, G., *Two Centuries of Virginia Cooking*. Amelia, Va.: Mid-South Pub., 1977.

Martineau, H., *Retrospect of Western Travel*, Vol. I. Sauders & Otly, 1838.

Nash, J.R., *Bloodletters and Badmen*. New York: Evans, 1973.

Novotony, A., *Strangers at the Door*. New York: Bantam, 1974.

Polonsky, J., *The Ghosts of Fort Monroe*. Hampton, Va.: Polyndrum Publications, 1972.

Randall, J.L., *Parapsychology and the Nature of Life*. New York: Harper & Row, 1975.

Roll, W.G., *Poltergeist*. New York: Signet, 1972.

Saltzman, P., *Ghosts and Other Strangers*. New York: Lancer, 1970.

Saxon, L., *Gumbo Ya-Ya*: A collection of Louisiana Folktales. Et Al Pub. by Folklore & Society, House Series, 1970, Lib. Bdg. Reprint, Chicago: Johnson, 1945.

Smith, E.T., *Psychic People*. New York: Bantam, 1968.

Smith, S., *Ghosts Around the House. World of the Strange.* New York: Pyramid, 1963. *Voices of the Dead.* New York: Signet, 1977. *The Book of James.* New York: Berkley Pub. Corp., 1974.

Snow, E.R., *Fantastic Folklore and Fact.* New York: Dodd, Mead, 1968.

Spraggett, A., *The Unexplained.* New York: New American Library, 1967.

Stambler & Landon, *Encyclopedia of Folk and Western Music.* Published, 1969.

Stearn, J., *The Door to the Future.* New York: MacFadden Books, 1963.

Steiger, Brad. *Real Ghosts.* Award Books, 1968.

Tackaberry, A., *Famous Ghosts, Phantoms, and Poltergeists for the Millions.* Nashville: Sherbourne Press, Inc., 1966.

Tralins, R., *The Hidden Spectre.* Script Associates, 1970.

Vetters, E.G., *Fabulous Frenchtown.* Coronet Press, 1955.

Wilkenson, F., *Firearms.* New York: Golden Press, 1973.

Williams, P., *The Supernatural.* London: Aldous Books, 1965.

Periodicals, Magazines, Journals and Newspapers

The Bakersfield Californian. Bakersfield, California; various issues.

Baltimore Sun. Baltimore, Maryland.

Beyond Reality. New York City. Various issues.

Fate Magazine. Various issues.

Fort Lauderdale News. Various issues.

The Hefley Report. June 1978.

The Jacksonville Journal, Jacksonville, Florida, May 12, 1978.

BIBLIOGRAPHY

The Miami News. March 7, 8, 1929.

The Nashville Banner. Various issues.

The Nashville Tennessean. Various issues.

Old Cars. February 8, 1977, and May 2, 1978.

Post-Dispatch Staff. Nashville, Tennessee. Various issues.

Probe Magazine. Various issues.

Rolling Stone. June 28, 1969. Ralph J. Gleason, "Perspective—Hank Williams, Roy Acuff and Then God!"

San Diego Squire, June 22, 1977.

The Springfield Union. Springfield, Massachusetts. Various issues.

Tennessee Historical Quarterly. Winter 1968.

Associated Press and United Press reports.

Index

238

ABOUT THE AUTHORS

Haunted Houses is RICHARD WINER's fourth book. His previous works are about mysteries of the sea, such as the bestseller *The Devil's Triangle*. He is presently working on several other books.

He is a graduate of the University of Minnesota and spent most of his working life in the news media and photography. He has also been a professional sailor, treasure hunter, yachtsman, hobo and soldier of fortune. His collection of vintage automobiles include a Pierce Arrow, several classic Packards, a Bugatti and some early sports racing cars. He is most often seen driving around Ft. Lauderdale in his everyday car—a red 1964 Corvette roadster.

NANCY MIDKIFF OSBORN was born August 26, 1939, in East Chicago, Indiana. She has been widowed for two years and has three children, Jack, Russ and Julie. Ms. Osborn resides in Pompano, Florida and has lived in southern Florida for ten years. Ms. Osborn attended Indiana University and Broward Community College, North campus, majoring in psychology. She has also attended the Arthur Ford Academy in Coral Gables, Florida and completed a course in parapsychology and mediumship. For more than eight years, Nancy Osborn has studied the paranormal in the laboratory and in the field. She gives lectures and does radio and TV appearances on topics of the supernatural. She welcomes letters and comments. Please be sure to enclose a stamped, self-addressed envelope if a reply is desired.

Bantam Book Catalog

Here's your up-to-the-minute listing of over 1,400 titles by your favorite authors.

This illustrated, large format catalog gives a description of each title. For your convenience, it is divided into categories in fiction and non-fiction—gothics, science fiction, westerns, mysteries, cookbooks, mysticism and occult, biographies, history, family living, health, psychology, art.

So don't delay—take advantage of this special opportunity to increase your reading pleasure.

Just send us your name and address and 50¢ (to help defray postage and handling costs).